The Dependency Curse

THE
DEPENDENCY
CURSE

*How Reliance on Government & Casinos
Damages Native American Lives*

JOE RIGERT

Copyright © 2016 by Joe Rigert

All rights reserved. No part of this publication may be reproduced or transmitted in any form or by any means, electronic or mechanical, including photocopy, recording, or any information storage and retrieval system now known or to be invented, without permission in writing from the publisher, except by a reviewer who wishes to quote brief passages in connection with a review written for inclusion in a magazine, newspaper, or broadcast.

CONTENTS

Introduction	1
Chapter I. Independent	11
Chapter II. Dependent	23
Chapter III. Independent?	39
Chapter IV. Terminated	59
Chapter V. Casino Dependency	75
Chapter VI. Klamaths Today	93
Chapter VII. Conclusion	109
Afterword	133
Postscript	160
Notes	163

INTRODUCTION

DECADES AGO, millions of African Americans migrated from South to North to escape oppression and find jobs. All the while, young people all over America have been leaving their rural farm homes to seek greater opportunities in the cities. At the same time, in a startling, little noticed migration, Native Americans have been doing the same, leaving their isolated reservations, established more than a century ago, to find better lives in mainstream urban America. Already, two-thirds of the natives have moved to small towns and cities, leaving behind what have become ghettos inhabited by people lacking jobs and dependent on government benefits.

Now, some native leaders are challenging this dependence, not only on government, but also on the riches of casino gambling. They see the dependence on government, a product of a vast reservation system, as a cause of a long-standing epidemic of social problems for their people. And they are concerned that a reliance on the unearned income from their casinos may contribute to those problems.

What do these challenges mean for the future of the five million original Americans? That is the question this author attempts to answer in this pioneering book, "The Dependency Curse," a compelling and controversial story, told for the first time, of how two wildly dissimilar Native American tribes suffer from the same malady: a dependency that saps their initiative to study and work. You could call it "A Tale of Two Tribes," a story featuring the Klamaths of Oregon and the Mdewakanton Sioux of Minnesota.

The Klamaths relied first on monthly payments from their timber sales and later became independent and wealthy upon selling their forests to the government. Then, after many had dissipated their one-time fortunes, they won back tribal status, dependent again on government benefits, prompting many to drink too much and work too little, but prompting others to seek better lives by joining the great migration from reservations to the cities.

At the other extreme, the Mdewakanton Sioux rose from poverty to build a gambling empire, making millions of dollars for members, year after year. In that tribe, adults don't have to work, and most don't. At the same time, young people looking forward to so much free money don't have to study and make something of their lives, and many of them don't do that either. Living on an extreme of unearned income, members of this tribe endure some of the same problems as the Klamaths, even more so.

This expression of concern over dependency is still small, but is gaining support, not from conservative white critics but from native leaders themselves. More than 50 years ago, venerated Klamath chairman Seldon Kirk didn't buy the romantic view of Indian Americans as eternal victims of white Europeans. Rather, he attributed their problems partly to a dependence on government payments from their timber sales. The Klamaths, he told this writer, had been coddled too long on those payments and had lost their initiative. Kirk knew because he had presided over the tribe as chairman in the four decades the members had been receiving those "per-capita" payments from the government, making them one of the most prosperous tribes in the country. [1]

Even then, Kirk lamented the difference in the status of whites and natives in the area. "I took a trip over the reservation a while ago," he said, "and saw much land, good houses, good fences and good crops. When I asked whose land it was, I learned that it was owned by the white man. The Indians' houses were run-down and shabby. It was a disappointment to me." The problems for his people went far beyond shabby homes, to include high

Introduction

prison rates, over half the children from broken homes, premature deaths from auto accidents, homicides and alcohol-related physical conditions. Not to mention low education levels and poor living conditions.

Like the Klamaths of Oregon, the Mdewakanton Sioux of Minnesota are dependent, too, but not on the government. They are dependent on the wealth of their gambling casino enterprise, a wealth that provides an unbelievable $1 million for each adult member each year, making them the wealthiest native tribe in the country, by far. That should make them an unmitigated success story, but it doesn't. In fact, for the Sioux, dependence on gaming could be viewed as a curse as well as a well-demonstrated cure. It has indeed produced tribal self-sufficiency. But as will be noted in this narrative it also has eliminated the incentive for the natives to get an education and a job, causing some to turn to drinking and drugs to compensate for empty lives. It has led to feuds and fights for control over the lucrative gambling business. It has caused a gambling addiction for some members. And it has led some young people to become undisciplined and spoiled, seeing no need to study or work.

Other natives on the 300 reservations in America have not been so "lucky" as to "enjoy" the mixed blessing of not working. Profound social problems, from suicides to alcohol addiction to parental neglect, have persisted during their continuing dependence on government benefits or on lesser casino profits. Kirk was ahead of his time in blaming dependency, at least in part, for native problems. Now other native leaders have joined the critique of the now-deceased Kirk as they seek a way out of a long-lasting social and economic depression. They don't call it a move for welfare reform, as imposed on the broader population, but in some ways that is what it is. And if it catches hold, it could have a profound effect on the lives of the original Americans.

But this writer is not so presumptuous as to claim that the native scholars and leaders he has chosen for their viewpoints on dependency represent a majority concern among the 5.2 million people in the native population. Others attribute the social ills to a possible genetic predisposition to a devastating addiction to alcohol, foisted on the natives in early years by white traders as trading bait. Or to a claimed disorder from a lingering trauma resulting from the loss of so much of their land and culture to European colonizers. Many, many natives, in fact, fiercely defend treaty rights to their remaining lands and resources, even at the cost of a dependence on government to maintain those rights.

A native scholar, Dr. Maria Yellow Horse Brave Heart, contends that the trauma—she doesn't mention dependency—contributes to a "current social pathology of high rates of suicide, homicide, domestic violence, child abuse, alcoholism and other social problems among American Indians."[2] The key words are "social pathology," reflected in large part by the Klamaths.

The subject is of more than passing interest to this writer. Of seven adopted children in our family of diverse races, two as Native Americans reflected the ills and strengths of their heritage. One died in her late 40s, unable to conquer a raging alcoholism that also had afflicted her birth parents. The other, Native American and African American, stopped drinking by sheer will power in his 20s and now, near 50, he is an outstanding city firefighter as well as a first-rate carpenter and mechanic, not to mention a mountain climber, youth hockey coach and, with his wife, a dedicated parent of three. Tellingly, he eschews racial identity, calling himself an American, a patriot. (I will add that he is intensely loyal to his family, not his tribe, though our family, in a way, is a tribe.)

Although we sought to build an appreciation of diversity in our family, race has not played an important part in the lives of our now-adult children, being superseded by the everyday problems and pleasures of life. Only one adopted family member, who is Mexican and Asian Indian, has tracked down and established a relationship with a birth parent (mother), though she also remains loyal to her adoptive parents. On the other hand, a granddaughter, who is one-quarter native, one-quarter African and half white, has shown an intense interest in her heritage, having many native friends in college and visiting a reservation as part of her studies in social work. She espouses a common view of Native Americans as victims of "white" government for loss of their land and much of their culture. As a demonstration of her beliefs, she is seeking enrollment in her Yakima tribe

Introduction

of Washington state in the hope of getting a job there as a social worker upon completion of her college work in that field. We admire her, even if we don't agree with all she believes. When I asked her if it bothered her that I challenged some of her opinions, she answered, "No, because I know I am right." But being right doesn't mean being of closed mind, espousing a romantic view of natives as eternal victims. She's learning about the real-world problems of native people, as she did recently in attending a big gathering in New Mexico. There a newly crowned "Miss Indian World" expressed a goal of contending with "a massive epidemic of suicides" among young people in her Great Sioux Nation. In her social work career, our granddaughter also will be dealing with that horrendous problem.

I mention all this family background, along with perspective derived from lots of reading and many native friendships, to make the point that my thinking, as portrayed in this book, also goes beyond the limits of race to encompass the diversity of opinion among natives themselves. And certainly, I do not pretend or want to speak for native people; I have left most of that to them.

And some are speaking out as never before. And that's the purpose of this book, to rely mostly on natives themselves, rather than "others," to speak about themselves and what is best for them. That means we will go beyond the "white" romanticism that views natives as close to nature and especially loving of children, that sees many of them as part of a hunting and fishing subsistence culture, that considers the answer to their problems is to regain, through constant legal battles, the land taken from them long ago. And to question the assertion that natives have a "treaty right" to regain reservation lands and retain government benefits in perpetuity regardless of the historic changes in their lives and circumstances. That is provocative, and so be it.

In making such sweeping goals for a book, this writer makes no pretense of being a sophisticated student of diverse cultures. Not sophisticated even though he and his spouse assembled a family of many ethnic and national backgrounds—black and native, Latina and Asian Indian, Japanese and Caucasian. Sophisticated? He remembers as a journalist referring to blacks as good as whites, considering whites the measuring standard, or to wampum and the Great White Father as the cliche language of the original Americans. But he has learned over the years to go beyond the stereotypes of the past and to go beyond race to see people, including his children, as all grappling with all the ups and downs of the "human" condition. (That is not to say that race is no longer a big deal in America, as shown in the recent deadly confrontations between white cops and unarmed young black men. or racism in the schools, or in attacks on Muslims.)

While this book addresses many of the issues applying to all the natives of America, the author, as noted, places a focus on only two tribes. The reasons for this focus are personal and professional. On a personal level, my wife came to know about the Klamaths when she lived in Klamath Falls near their reservation. In her early years, she heard about the successful native ranchers as a contrast to the native alcoholics staggering on the streets of town—a contrast we have seen in our family. From a professional standpoint, I learned about the Klamaths while working on the Klamath Falls newspaper and while writing about them as a reporter at the now-defunct Oregon Journal in Portland. And as long-time residents in Minneapolis, we both read the many accounts of the nearby Mdewakanton Sioux, the tribe of millionaires, and have learned about them from a grandson, who is friend of a tribal member.

Though the Klamaths are far from wealthy, they are distinctive historically, dating back perhaps more than 12,000 years. They also were fortunate in not being forced by the government to relocate to alien territory, as were many tribes across the country. They stayed on what would become a forest fortune, much as a few other tribes became wealthy from coal and oil on their reservations. Mindful of their past, moreover, the Klamaths remain dedicated to this day to maintaining "the customs and heritage" of their ancestors.[3] But like most tribes, the Klamaths illustrate the changing fortunes of America's natives, they having lived through the extremes, reflecting in part the changes in federal policies applying only to natives, as well as the social and economic changes affecting all Americans.

In the early 1800s, the Klamaths lived independently by raising horses and counting on wild game, fish and native plants for food. In the 1900s,

Introduction

after being forced to live on their reservation, they relied later on the payments from the government's annual sales of their timber. Then, in the 1960s, in a controversial decision to end the federal dependence of certain tribes, the government took ownership of the Klamath timber and paid most of the native people for it, making instant millionaires, in today's dollars, of each family. But that one-time fortune didn't last for some tribal members unprepared to handle sudden wealth and, at their insistence, the government restored its control over their lives. As a result, they now depend again on government aid, without income from sales of timber they no longer own. Today, more than 3,670 people still consider themselves as tribal members, whether on their reservation or off. That's triple the number of years past.

On the other hand, the Mdewakanton Sioux, a tiny tribe of less than 500 people, was part of the powerful Dakota nation that, in the 1860s, was defeated and dispersed by the government to nearby states and Canada in their futile fight to maintain their homelands.[4] The Mdewakanton tribe was allowed to remain in Minnesota because it sided with the government in the uprising.[5] But for more than 100 years thereafter, its members endured the poverty of dirt roads, inadequate housing and food subsidies. That changed dramatically in the late 1900s when their leaders saw an opportunity in the emerging Indian gaming industry, and turned it into a tribal fortune. Their great fortune was made possible by a monopoly for Indian gambling, granted by the government for many tribes across the country. The monopoly allowed the Sioux to exploit, without competition, a huge market of "customers" within the Twin Cities metropolitan area. So now each of the Sioux natives is "dependent" on $1 million a year from the unprecedented profits of their casino gambling. And with so much "free" money, almost nobody works, tribal chairman Stanley Crooks told the New York Times. That's right, 99 percent unemployment by choice, he said.[6] (Crooks has since died of a lung illness at age 70.)

In neither case, however, have the benefits of dependence, whether on government or gambling, or an imposed independence, solved the social problems of tribal members. In fact, it could be argued—heretically perhaps—that living in the fiction of independent sovereign nations—the reservation system itself—where there is too little employment and too much dependence, has helped create a culture, not of independence, but of failure. And that culture, presumably perpetuated in the reservation ghettos, has followed many of the natives in their continuing migration to the cities, where most of them are now living. Like the African Americans who moved north for jobs after slavery, Native Americans are moving to the cities for the same reason.

As for the Klamaths, chairman Kirk went way back to recall good times. "It was good when everyone realized that he had to work. Most of the Indians built houses, had cows and pigs…Those were the nice days, and we were happy then." Kirk worked, too, after attending schools away from the reservation, first becoming a tribal policeman and then working for years as a carpenter, even building a house for himself. Of course, many of us have nostalgic views of the "good old days," and Kirk was no exception, because as we will note, the old days for the Klamaths weren't all good.

And they would get less good. When the Klamaths became a dependent people, dependent on the cash payments, many of the parents quit working, according to Kirk. That was the start of a dependency that some natives, like Kirk decades ago, blame for the social problems that persist even today for the Klamaths and many Native Americans across the country. For many Klamaths, the "free" money had not solved the problems, but rather had exacerbated them.

Amazingly, Kirk's views on the disability of dependence were echoed the other day by an Army officer on the front page of the New York Times. Lt. Col. Daniel Gade contended that disability checks for troops injured in war might actually be harmful. Too many veterans, he said, become financially dependent on the monthly checks, choose not to find jobs and lose the sense of identity and self-worth that can come from work. Speaking to sick and wounded soldiers at an army base, Gade said, "People who stay home because they are getting paid enough to get by on disability are worse off. They are more likely to abuse drugs and alcohol. They are more likely to live alone." Better to offer incentives for them to find work or create businesses, he said.

Introduction

Indeed, those words stand the test of time, especially coming from people like Kirk and Gade, who speak from experience.

Like Kirk, Gade had credibility to express these concerns; he's a professor at the U.S. Military Academy and a combat veteran who lost a leg while serving as a tank commander in Iraq in 2005. Some veterans advocates say Gade is siding with fiscal conservatives who want to reduce federal spending, even if at a cost to wounded veterans. And some Native American advocates have argued that any efforts to curtail their dependency relationship with the government is a violation of longstanding treaties with the U.S. government compensating for the taking of their land. On the contrary, it could be argued, as posed in this book, that living in the fiction of independent sovereign nations—the reservation system itself—where there is too little employment and too much dependence, has helped create a culture, not of independence, but of failure. And that culture, presumably perpetuated in the reservation ghettos, has followed many of the natives in their continuing migration to the cities, where more than two-thirds of them are now living. Like the African Americans who moved north for jobs after slavery, Native Americans are moving to the cities for the same reason.

These are some, but hardly all, of the issues to be discussed in this book. The writer will also consider the profound irony of government policy in the late 1800s, freeing the slaves in the South, while making prisoners of the Klamaths in the North, requiring them to get government permission to leave, temporarily, their so-called reservation (and no whites allowed in at first). He will relate the rebellious response of one of the Klamath tribes, the Modoc people going to war in an heroic effort to regain their homeland, the Klamaths breaking the government rules by cutting and selling the timber that originally belonged to them, not the government. And he will describe the bumbling—and unsuccessful—efforts of the government overlords to make farmers out of the people in terrain unsuitable for farming.

Most of all, the writer will seek to show the ambiguities of the people, whether going to war or forming a peace party, functioning mostly out of self-interest, as do most people at all times in all places.

CHAPTER I

Independent

THE GOOD LIFE? Independent and self-sufficient? That's one version of how it was for Native Americans, including the Klamaths of Oregon, before the government took away much of their land and forced them onto reservations. That's the way fur trapper Peter Skeen Ogden, the first white man in 1826 to visit the Klamaths, saw them: honest, friendly and satisfied with their lot in life. They were well supplied with the fish upon which they depended for their livelihood. With the condescension by which dominant people often refer to the poor, he went on to say they were a "happy race whose wants are so few and live happy and contented with such miserable food and I may add live and die independent of others." (Ogden predicted that the Klamaths would not remain honest and friendly when deprived of their independent lives. "Two years intimacy with the whites will make them like all other Indians villains," he wrote.)[1]

Certainly the Klamaths did not consider their food miserable. One of the most important crops was pond-lily seeds known as wokas, which they harvested in the marshes. It was so important that the native shamans, or medicine men, would perform rituals in late summer to assure a plentiful crop.[2] Later, in a showing of colonial arrogance, government agents sought to suppress the native religion and supplant it with the Methodist belief

The Dependency Curse

system founded in England (actually a decent religion that sought prison reform and opposed slavery). Of course, the Klamaths were not always satisfied with their lives, despite Ogden's facile observation. They were forced to eat boiled or roasted animal hides if their food supplies ran out in a long winter. Moreover, Ogden conceded that at times of famine and fear, the natives resorted to thievery to satisfy their needs.

And thievery was the least of it, especially after the arrival of the white settlers in the 1840s. You'll find another view of their early lives in the reports of the U.S. commissioners of Indian affairs, from the priceless collections of the National Archives in Washington, D.C. You'll learn of wars among the natives, even within tribes. Of the taking of slaves to sell for horses. Of whites killing natives and natives killing whites, sometimes in massacres on both sides.

Yes, wars among the natives. As one Indian affairs commissioner reported in 1854: "The Klamaths were once numerous, but wars with the surrounding tribes, and conflicts among themselves, have rendered them weak. They now number but four hundred and fifteen souls… Their lodges are generally mere temporary structures, scarcely sheltering them from the pelting storm. Some of them have visited the (white) settlements and obtained tents, camp equipage and clothing. They possess a few horses, and among them I saw four guns, but they had no ammunition. The bow and arrow, knife, and war-club, constitute their weapons."2

In some ways, however, those wars in the early 1800s were profitable. Scholar Theodore Stern quotes Klamath Chief Chiloquin as saying, "We found we could make money by war, for we sold the provisions and property captured for horses and other things we needed. It was like soldiers nowadays who fight for money. We made war because we made money by it and we rather got to like it anyhow."

And then there was the taking of slaves. "In 1843," according to Stern, "one missionary recorded the visit of 'a large party of the Klamath tribe, fierce and warlike…with about twenty slaves (who) sold most or all of them. Some, I was informed were sold for three horses each, some cheaper.'" No, the buying and selling of slaves was not confined to the American South.

I. Independent

This account by Stern, in his seminal history of the Klamaths, concluded that though the native cultures at that time made possible a good life in which dignity and worth had a place, those were not the "halcyon days sometimes depicted today." Stern quotes Klamath leader Henry Blow on how the Klamath territory was a "bad country," some men stealing property and squaws, killing tribesmen who resisted, creating a climate of might was right. The comments almost certainly exaggerated the conditions, says Stern, but still possessed an essential truth.

The chronicles of the times do portray the brutality of early life: As in their battles with surrounding tribes, or as in the Klamaths taking slaves to sell for cherished horses from other tribes—a lucrative traffic. As one historian writes, the Klamaths would stage regular raids of another tribe, "surround the camps, kill the men and abduct the women and children in their homes, or sell them into slavery."[3] (It should be noted that tribal conflict has hardly been confined to the Klamaths or other native tribes long ago, as shown today in the battles of "religious tribes" in the Middle East and Africa.)

By the 1850s, the Klamaths traded atrocities with the white settlers, described by the Indian affairs officials as "outrages" in the killing of whites and natives suffering from disease and hunger. "The early settlers of the country everywhere met with a kind reception from the Indians," said a commissioner in 1864, "but as the settlements increased in numbers and extended their borders, it soon became manifest to the Indians that their hunting grounds were being invaded and their limits gradually restricted. Their feelings of hospitality were in time changed to sentiments of bitterest hostility, and that dark page of our national history, containing a recital of our numerous Indian wars, and the peculiarly bloody and barbarous scenes attending them, has been the result."[4]

Indeed, in the bloody and barbarous scenes of the "Indian wars," native warriors killed more than 70 white settlers in three separate attacks in the late 1840s[5], and, in turn, a decade later, a party of white settlers massacred 40 natives under a flag of truce.[6] In the middle of all this, as victims and aggressors, were Modoc Indians, sometimes enemies of the Klamaths, who

The Dependency Curse

were forced to live on the Klamath reservation, and in rebellion went to war against the U.S. Army. The Modocs were defeated after four months of battle, during which time they killed unarmed U.S. General Edward Canby, a Civil War hero, during peace talks.[7] (You'll find more references to the Modoc war throughout this narrative; it is highly important.)

(War is hell is the cliché, but it rings true with all its attendant atrocities throughout history. I remember a health official in Washington state telling me how in World War II he watched sailors on his Navy ship shooting and killing Japanese Navy men in the water below screaming to be saved. None were.)

So now we arrive at the question: What led the U.S. government to take over control of the Klamaths and make them a dependent people? The answer, again, can be found in part in the reports of the U.S. commissioners of Indian affairs, the reports written at the peak of the conflict between whites and Indians. By 1862, writes one commissioner, white settlers and miners, in their inexorable push West, were complaining forcefully about the Indians in Oregon, urging the government to extinguish Indian title to the lands and open them up to settlement.[8]

And the Klamaths, in their own view of the past, were complaining about the invasion of the white Europeans. "The (white) trespassers swarmed over our sacred ancestral land, putting up fences, clearing lands and killing and/or frightening away wildlife," they wrote later. "The rush for gold brought even more intruders, eager to take what they could. Our people, like any people protecting their homeland, resisted these invaders who were violating our way of life. In the end, in spite of our efforts to protect land and resources, the non-Indian culture prevailed. Plagued by disease brought in by the settlers and weakened by continuous battle, the Klamaths, Modocs and Yahooskin Band of Snake Indians entered into the Treaty of 1864."[9] The treaty forced them all to live on the Klamath homeland, which had been severely reduced in size.

In summary, was it bad white invaders vs. good native defenders of their land? Donald Fixico, an Arizona State University professor who counts four tribes in his background, writes that it was more complicated than that.

I. Independent

Humanitarians, he writes, felt that the United States was responsible for preserving Indian existence and initiated a reform movement to aid in the recovery of the defeated natives. In 1850, he notes, the commissioner of Indian Affairs requested the relocation of western tribes to reservations for their self-preservation. "Federal bureaucrats argued that the reservation program would protect Indians from white depredations and that they would receive needed supplies to survive in a sedentary life-style."[10] (Making them dependent, of course.)

Whatever the stated rationale for the federal Indian policy of forcing natives to live on reservations, it led to armed native opposition and that, says Fixico, led to a nationwide suppression of the Indian population. But the government had not sought to defeat and move the natives by military force alone. For one thing, the country was involved in a horrendous civil war in the east that was requiring millions of soldiers and taking the lives of hundreds of thousands of them. It apparently preferred to avoid a costly and protracted war in the West against the Indians. Besides that, government agents did not underestimate the prowess of the natives, and knew from experience they would not go down without a fight. According to one of their reports, "The Klamath Lake and Modoc Indians number about fourteen hundred warriors, all well mounted on Indian ponies, and armed with guns, and are skilful marksmen; are large, active, and courageous Indians and would make formidable foes; and many of our straggling citizens in the early days of the country have fallen victim to them."[11]

But one government officer, Col. Charles Drew, was not to be deterred. He was suspected of "endeavoring, through harsh measures, to foment a general Indian war which would divert much needed troops from the fighting on the eastern seaboard" (thus favoring the South). Rational thinkers in the government branded him a "Copperhead," meaning one of the northern Democrats who opposed the Civil War.[12]

Drew did not prevail. In fact, according to one report, the Indians were considered to be part of separate nations rather than enemy combatants. The report elaborated: "As our borders have been extended, and civilization with its attendant blessings has taken possession of the once unbroken

The Dependency Curse

wilderness home of the Indians, treaties have been negotiated with them from time to time, and uniformly…they have been recognized as a separate and distinct people, possessing in a restricted sense the peculiarities and characteristics of distinct nations."[13]

The answer for the Klamaths would be to negotiate a treaty to achieve a peaceful solution to the conflict. This treaty of 1864 would not, however, treat the natives as equals in a separate nation. It would take away much of their territory and render them dependent on the government overlords. The treaty, in fact, declared that the Klamaths "acknowledge their dependence upon the government of the United States." On its part, the government would pay the natives small amounts of money to "promote" their well-being, "advance them in civilization…and to secure their moral improvement and education." And "help" them become farmers.[14]

The government, as reflected in the commissioner reports, felt well justified in subjugating the natives in view of their many "murders" of white settlers beginning with the arrival of wagon trains in 1846 and continuing thereafter. In 1863, a commissioner referred to the natives as "a horde of piratical thieves, highwaymen and murderers, cowardly sycophants before the white man's face, and perfidious assassins behind his back." It was a telling description of how at least one government agent viewed what could be seen as guerrilla warfare by the Klamath tribes to maintain their homeland. Even then, a commissioner the next year conceded that it was necessary to provide 9,921 pounds of beef, 11,401 pounds of flour and other articles of subsistence to suffering natives, not only on humane grounds, but also to keep them from stealing food from the whites. Besides that, the commissioner wrote, helping the Klamaths "had a most salutary effect on conciliating the Indians, and rendering future control of them easy and economical."[15]

The key word there is "control." And in the beginning, after the treaty was signed that year of 1864, it looked as if control was assured. In the words of an Indian affairs official, Elijah Steele, "all (the Klamaths) had learned to both fear and respect me, and they readily assembled in council, and were evidently highly gratified at a restoration of peace among themselves and a

I. Independent

good understanding with us. Since this arrangement, it has been proven by actual experience that they intend fully to comply with the terms of the compact. Their guns were all kept back on their visit...after the treaty, and individual white men have passed into their country and back without molestation or annoyance."[16]

Meantime, some of the native leaders, who had lived with whites and worked for white farmers, had become convinced that the best policy for the Klamaths was one of peace, thus becoming leaders not only of their tribe but also of a "peace party."[17] As one leader explained, "Even if they felt like avenging the death of the (Klamath) people, they knew they could not contend against the whites long, for they had learned they (whites) were as numerous as the trees on the mountains."[18]

Yet, the fear and respect, as patronizingly described, didn't last. One faction of the natives actually began a campaign to kill the whites.[19] And the negotiated peace treaty itself would lead to war. The treaty required the Modoc tribe to leave its homeland to the south and live on the reservation with the Klamaths. The Modocs, near starvation in alien territory, refused to bow to the will of government and rose up in rebellion less than a decade later. It was a war of independence, a war to avoid dependence. One of the Modoc leaders was Schonchin John, who earlier had been praised by the government for being "smart, sober and well-disposed."

The Modoc war was one of dozens of native uprisings that continued across the West until the end of the 19th century, showing that the Indians were not to be passively subdued. The original Americans inflicted heavy losses on civilians as well as the military as they sought to retain their territories. And they suffered even heavier losses in their battles with the far superior forces of the invading white government. Remember the 1890 Battle of Wounded Knee, a massacre in which the Army killed 150 Sioux Indians.

It was no wonder the Modocs rebelled. The Klamaths retained the core of their homeland in the new reservation, and acted as lords of the land toward the southern newcomers, treating them as if they were there only on sufferance, according to Stern in his history of the Klamaths. "Captain Jack

The Dependency Curse

(another Modoc leader) is reported to have told his followers, 'I do not want my men to be slaves for these Indians, and they shall not be. My people are just as good as these Indians.'"[20]

Even then, Schonchin John signed the treaty with the government, having undergone a change of heart. "I thought if we killed all the white men we saw, that no more would come. We killed all we could; but they came more and more like new grass in the spring. I looked around and saw that many of our young men were dead and could not come back to fight. My heart was sick. My people were few. I threw down my gun. I said, 'I will not fight again. I made friends with the white man.'"[21]

But Schonchin's change of heart came at a price. As a result, he was estranged from the tribe and came under pressure from hawkish members in a classic example of political conflict (like today?). So, in the parlance of today, he flip-flopped and joined in the rebellion to regain his leader status. Later he was accused of taking part in the killing of the unarmed general Canby and a minister. After bitter fighting, the government forces, vastly outnumbering the natives, and with help from the rival Warm Springs tribe, put down the uprising, executed Schonchin and three other Modocs and shipped their followers to Oklahoma.[22]

Enlisting members of a rival tribe to fight an "Indian" war against the Modocs? It was not unusual, any more than it was unusual for the government to rely on tribal enemies of the powerful Comanches to serve as army scouts in the battle to subdue the Comanches in the Southwest. (So much for the myth of a monolithic "Indian" race, acting together of one mind.) Oh yes, the U.S. government relied on Sunnis to contend with Shiites in Iraq, and then saw the roles reversed, this being more than a century later. It's all part of the ebb and flow of history.

Back to the Modoc war, in an ultimate insult to Schonchin, the U.S. army forced him to sign a paper that read, "Signature of the Modoc chief the evening before his execution." The document is kept in the Klamath County Museum as a relic of a native uprising that made headlines across America and Europe.[23]

Today, Lynn Schonchin a direct descendent of Schonchin John, a high

I. Independent

school history teacher, refers to all of his Modoc ancestors as "freedom fighters, as patriots, as much as Washington and Jefferson; they were fighting for freedom and their own homeland. I do not see them as warriors; I see them as men fighting for their homeland." In an interview, this writer asked Schonchin why the government executed the Modoc leaders and not any other native rebels in the "Indian wars." His answer: "Because they killed Canby; he was the only general killed in a war (Indian war) and when you have 40 to 50 Modocs who held off the army as long as they did, that was embarrassing. And if you look at the trial, most of the men in the court martial trial, Canby was their commander. It supposedly was a hearing for war crimes. John Schonchin (shot) Meacham (a government official) but he didn't die. (Captain) Jack killed Canby."[24]

Is he bitter? "Yeah. I could let it eat at me. No matter what I would be in life, I could never hold a candle to what those people did. The courage, those things they left us, fighting for their own home and families, positive things. They are things I have to live by. I look at the positive things." But some things are not positive for the Klamaths, says Schonchin, noting that when his daughter went to a store; the guys in there were swearing at the tribe about their treaty fishing rights. "She told them, 'I am one of those Indians and I respect those who fish.' They started making fun of her. They are ranchers living on free land, and that girl's ancestors gave up their lives (for her)." Schonchin also cited the bumper strips, "Save the salmon, kill the Indians."

"Here very few Indians can get jobs," Schonchin continued. "Those that do hire Indians, their prices are higher, but I go there. As a kid, I was just as bad, I did not want to have anything to do with them (whites). Prejudice against whites is wrong. My grandkids know who they are. I have never heard them use terminology that is negative about people. I have taught my grandkids, don't be angry about race, it's individuals, my grandmother said, 'nobody is better than you and you are no better than anybody else. My step granddad told the kids, all work is honorable.'"

Many whites are not so open-minded now, and they certainly weren't a century ago when an Indian-affairs commissioner declared that the natives "should be subjugated and governed like a colony." In other words, the Klamaths, including the Modocs, would not be living in a free, independent nation. They would be subjugated, dependent on the government. [25]

The Modoc war was one small part of the government campaign to subjugate native people across America. The army of regulars and volunteers fought hundreds of battles against the natives in the 1700s and 1800s—with massacres and atrocities on both sides—until wars and treaties brought them all under control, living in reservation ghettos, living dependently.

During this time, many of the natives had also become dependent in another way, on the debilitating effects of alcohol. In his book, "The Roots of Dependency," historian Richard White writes that the French and English—especially the English— introduced alcohol to the Choctaw nation to increase trade in animal pelts, a major commodity sought by the Europeans. Before that, the southeastern tribe subsisted on venison and agriculture.[26]

Once liquor was available, the Choctaw hunted for rum, not for needed clothes and tools, creating a growing dependence on the English. The dependence was exacerbated by the imposition of credit, putting the natives in debt and increasing the pressure to hunt to repay their debts. "Whiskey remained the bane of the Choctaw nation," White wrote. "Missionaries reported that they never saw violence between Choctaw men unless the participants were drunk, but then the affrays became murderous. Liquor did not kill most Choctaw, however; it merely impoverished them.[27]

(Since the bad days, the Choctaw have brought about an amazing recovery, now operating six businesses, seven casinos, eight health clinics, even building their own hospital. The tribe did this after having been forced to relocate west to Oklahoma, traveling with other native people, including Cherokee tribal members, on the deadly Trail of Tears, which will be discussed later.)

The Klamaths also have suffered from the liquor scourge. White traders sold them liquor in exchange for money that government agents had given them for the treaty purchase of their land. These white men, eager to exploit the Klamaths, followed in the footsteps of the agents to encourage them to

I. Independent

squander their money on whiskey, tobacco and trinkets, according to an Indian-affairs commissioner.[28] Stern noted that a government agent also "inveighed against 'a low class of white men living near the reservation who have been giving and selling liquor to the Indians.'"[29]

Today, for many Native Americans (and many other Americans), alcohol remains a debilitating disease, a pathology, that causes early death, traffic accidents, crime and greater dependence.

CHAPTER II

Dependent

AN ALCOHOL DEPENDENCY? It wasn't supposed to be that way. Under the treaty of 1864, the government provided that "if any member of these tribes shall drink any spirituous liquor, or bring any such liquor upon the reservation, his or her proportion of the benefits of this treaty may be withheld for such time as the President of the United States may direct."[1] The treaty did not mention the role of the white "citizens" in bringing liquor to the natives. Of course, the prohibition did not stick, any more than it would for the nation as a whole years later.

And what were those treaty benefits at risk? Small annual payments for the vast amounts of land taken from the natives, along with equipment and services for farming, a flour mill, manual-labor school and medical facilities The treaty also provided a sawmill, which was a significant benefit for the Klamaths, as will be explained later. Beyond that the natives were given the exclusive right to hunt, fish and gather natural food on their reservation. It was the least the government could do for them, and it was the least, considering what they had given up.

The liquor prohibition was obviously a small part of the treaty. Most significant of all was the language spelling out the status of the Klamaths, more or less as children, subservient to their parent government, forbidden to fight among themselves or with American citizens. This is worth quoting

The Dependency Curse

in full: "Article ⁹. The several tribes of Indians, parties to this treaty, acknowledge their dependence upon the government of the United States, and agree to be friendly with all citizens thereof, and to commit no depredations upon the person or property of said citizens, and to refrain from carrying on any war upon other Indian tribes." Note the reference to "citizens," meaning the European occupiers but not the original American natives, who didn't get to be citizens until six decades later.[2]

The language of the treaty makes it clear that a major purpose of the agreement, from the standpoint of the government, was to protect the white settlers. As a commission appointed by Congress to look into a boundary dispute would put it later, "It was evidently a principal object of the treaty to draw the Indians in from the large extent of territory over which they were roaming, subject to constant collisions with the steadily encroaching whites, and concentrate them in an area much more limited, but would still be ample to provide them with the means of subsistence."[3] To make the point explicitly, the treaty also declared, without equivocation, that the natives were forbidden to leave without permission from the government agent. What about the claim, stated earlier, that the purpose of the agreement also was a humanitarian effort to protect the natives from the whites? Granted, whites were not to be allowed to "locate or remain" upon the reservation, but the treaty did not stop some from moving onto reservation lands, causing conflicts with natives who viewed them as interlopers. The government intervened to enforce the treaty, and properly so.

Much later, in 1938, the U.S. Supreme Court affirmed what was obvious: The United States had power to control and manage the affairs of its Indian wards in good faith for their welfare…subject to constitutional limitations." (The author would add, and the welfare of the encroaching whites.)

For the original Americans across the country, eventual defeat in their guerrilla "wars" and forced acceptance of a reservation system had made them wards of the government much earlier, no longer free to live their lives as they wished, or to live where they wanted. As we have noted, the 1864 treaty with the Klamaths required them to obtain permission from a

II. Dependent

government agent to leave the reservation. After the Modoc war in the late 1800s, the government had tightened the controls, demanding a signed pass to leave.[4] Sure, whites were to be expelled if they entered the reservation, but they otherwise were free to settle where they wished, without fear any more of attacks by natives.

The same was true nationally. A plethora of government treaties with native tribes opened up and protected travel routes through Indian territories and protected tribes from reprisal attacks by white settlers. Native author David Treuer summarizes the treaty period, lasting from 1851 to 1871, this way: "The U.S. government made treaties with Indians for two main reasons. First, the United States had to make treaties, because Indian tribes were powerful. They had command of routes of travel, many warriors and plenty of resources when the United States had very little of any of these. The second reason was cynical: paper was cheaper than bullets. Despite the power of Indian tribes, it was often the case that the United States had no intention of honoring the treaties it made. Treaties were a way to reduce the power of the tribes."[5]

Treuer makes a good case for that rationale. Another critic went farther to contend that the government was enforcing red apartheid, similar to the one-time controls over blacks in South Africa. The Klamaths were bottled up in a reservation ghetto. The blacks of Africa were confined to "homelands" until the late Nelson Mandela, after spending 27 years in prison, led the way for his people—an overwhelming majority of the country's population—to take control of the government, when the minority whites recognized they could no longer maintain their domination. By contrast, the natives of America are a tiny minority and know they cannot supplant the white majority.

On or off a reservation, however, life could have been worse for the Klamaths. Like many people in early times, they were living off the land, adequately or not, before moving on to better livelihoods. Former tribal chairman Jeff Mitchell wrote in 1996 how the natives would catch and dry 50 tons of fish each year, how he would harvest up to a dozen deer per year, how he would go with grandparents to dig for roots for storage and use in the winter, how they would gather pond lilly seeds to grind into flour, how they would go to a mountain to gather berries. "This was the cycle we followed year after year," he wrote. As part of their culture, the Klamaths shared their bounty with other tribal members in need, he said.[6]

According to another account, the Klamaths also were hunting bear, coyotes, wolves and various other fur-bearing animals that furnished blankets and clothing. Further, they killed geese, ducks and other birds, also used for food and for feather blankets and clothes. The natives had ingenious ways to hunt and fish, using flares to attract waterfowl, ambushing game from pits, smoking bear out of their dens, even disguising themselves by wearing animal heads and entire skins.[7]

Later, however, many of the traditional foods, as well as the fish and game, were drastically depleted. Depleted or not, Mitchell didn't say how many of the Klamaths in the 20th century wanted to or could continue to rely on such a subsistence way of life. Yet, as late as 1996 the Klamaths contended in a lawsuit that the tribes depended on mule deer, not just for their subsistence, but also for their "way of life." (As though they wanted a diet of deer meat.}

The assertions on "subsistence" came in that legal dispute between the tribes and the government over whether the planned harvesting of old-growth tribal forests would reduce the deer population and thereby negatively affect their treaty right to hunt and fish. (The tribes said the timber harvesting hurt the deer habitat; the government said, persuasively, that it helped by creating more edible undergrowth.) But this debate seems a bit moot considering the question of whether the deer supply was really that important for the tribes in the modern times of the late 20th century. It was also somewhat moot because Klamath biologist Craig Bienz had declared in that dispute that "many of the species which the tribes historically harvested for subsistence purposes were no longer available for them to hunt and fish. Nearly all of them, he said, were either endangered, in significant decline or completely absent from the former reservation lands.[8]

Leaving behind that diversion in this stage of our narrative, we should re-emphasize, in all fairness, that the treaty of 1864 was not all bad for the

II. Dependent

Klamaths, even though it deprived them of most of the 21 million acres they had claimed as their territory—a significant claim for any country anywhere. The Klamath treaty assured the tribal members not only of the right to hunt, fish and gather plant food on their reservation, but, as noted earlier, also provided assistance to help them "adopt an agricultural way of life." The language of the treaty is instructive: continuing payments to the tribes for their land was to be "expended...to promote the well-being of the Indians, advance them in civilization, and especially agriculture, and to secure their moral improvement and education."[9]. A federal court would conclude that one of the essential purposes in setting aside the Klamath reservation, was to encourage the Indians to take up farming." (This was the beginning of a dependency that would grow in the years to come.)

Of course, while hunting and fishing were needed to maintain a short-term subsistence culture, they would hardly assure the thousands of Klamaths a livelihood in the years ahead (see above). As for farming, it may have represented a way of life for some of the government treaty-makers, but it was just as impractical for the Klamaths in the short run as the hunting and fishing guarantee was for the long future. A government boundary commission would write later that "there is no provision in the treaty...for the support of the Indians by the government, and as the high altitude and the severity of the climate are unfavorable to the cultivation of cereals, their subsistence depended upon natural products, consisting principally of game, fish, wild roots and seeds."[10]

Nevertheless, the government agents had persisted in their efforts to turn the natives into farmers. Their goal, a worthy one, was to make them self-supporting, not dependent on the government—possibly within 20 years. Rather than sow the seeds of dependency, they would plant the roots of independence. To accomplish this, they first sought to enlist the Klamaths voluntarily to work the land. When that failed to attract enough "farmers," they decided, unbelievably, to enlist the aid of the military and police to encourage and induce them, even school teachers and boys, to grow an agricultural society.[11]

It was an amazing experiment of a government trying to run the lives of the original Americans, by forcing them to live on a reserve, and to leave only with permission, and by inducing them to adopt a certain way of life, a farming life, in a hostile environment. It was even worse than the forced settlement of the farmers of the Soviet Union, now Russia, in the commune system that would be imposed later. In an implicit recognition of the doomed system of containment on the reservation, the government allowed many of the Klamaths to go outside to work for white farmers or to run trucking businesses to carry supplies for the government agency.

The failure to develop a self-supporting community of native farmers in this corner of America is described in great detail by anthropologist Stern in his history of the Klamaths, published a half-century ago. His work is based on original documents, letters and commentaries, primarily of the government. It's a balanced, realistic portrayal of an impossible struggle to mold people to a preconceived way of life.

In the first year of this forced farming, the crops were reported to be good. But after that they were killed by frosts or summer droughts, or suffered from heavy frosts along with unprecedented heat, this on a semi-arid plateau 4,000 feet above sea level. The government agents were not to be deterred, wrote Stern. Surveying blighted fields, they redoubled their efforts, enlisting even teachers to spend a greater part of their time on the farms, along with Indian boys receiving instruction on manual labor.[12]

When other agents one after another failed in this effort, still another sallied into the fray, as chronicler Stern put it. A new government administrator, an agricultural college professor, insisted that "agriculture can be made a comparative success," falsely blaming his predecessors for not offering encouragement. In short, this time the new guy would "encourage" the natives to be independent, not dependent. And if that didn't work? See below.

If the Indians would not farm on their own, by damn, administrator Joseph Emery would force them to. At his behest, the Indian police "assisted in the general order that all able-bodied Indians will be required to do some work in agriculture." (The Chinese tried that, remember?) Alas, after the second year, when nine-tenths of the Klamaths had been induced to work

II. Dependent

in the fields, unprecedented heat prompted Emery to move on to "greener pastures." The severity of the climate, as predicted, had deterred him. But he persisted, resuming his forced farming program when he returned for another government tour 10 years later. That's true.

No wonder Emery failed. Four successive government agents had preceded him in the defeat of the farming effort. (They were all slow learners, and as a college professor, he knew better.) Two had warned him of the farming futility (if he read their reports.) Capt. O.C. Knapp declared, "I again urge upon the department the uselessness of trying to make this an agricultural reservation...The Indians should be supplied with cattle and sheep, and they would soon become self-sustaining." Agent L. S. Dyar wrote that "these (crop) failures are very discouraging to the Indians as well as to the agent, and demonstrate the necessity of paying more attention to the raising of cattle."[13]

And the government did, redirecting its emphasis to the raising of cattle. Agent Linus Nickerson, who had met defeat in farming before Emery, reported that 2,000 head of cattle had been introduced to the reservation during his tenure. Some of the Klamaths were raising cattle for market, enabling them to make enough money to supply necessities. Within five years, he claimed, ten times that number could be carried by the reservation, to make the tribe entirely self-supporting. Except, a severe winterkill the next year destroyed three-quarters of the cattle and 40 percent of the horses.[14] Nature took its toll, as usual.

Despite that setback, Stern reported, the stock-raising program slowly recovered, prompting the government to turn farming increasingly to the production of hay to feed the cattle in winter. The government started to buy beef for its employees, as well as to promote beef sales to buyers as far away as San Francisco. Under the impetus of this demand, Nickerson noted, a "considerable number of enterprising Indian families...are taking up fencing stock ranches." That was some 20 years after the reservation was established.[15] Well into the next century, prosperous native ranches were part of the agricultural economy of the area, as attested by my spouse who lived in nearby Klamath Falls in her early years.

The Dependency Curse

From farming to cattle ranching, the government kept trying to make the Klamath reservation system a success, without success. The next effort, on a national scale that also affected the Klamaths, was to allow natives under the so-called federal Dawes act to take ownership of plots of land. Under this ingenious plan the natives would have the incentive to make the best use of their land, whether farming or ranching. That effort also failed. One reason, according to economists W. T. Trulove and David Bunting, was that the Klamaths did not have the resources to invest in agricultural pursuits.[16] Additionally, the natives also were allowed to sell or lease their land to white farmers, which many of them did for quick income, thereby reducing by more than two-thirds the land allotted to them. In short, they found another way to be dependent on unearned income, with no work on their part.

Critics, meantime, saw the Dawes or "allotment" act as a greedy move to get Indian land and open it up to white settlement. Reformers, on the other hand, saw it as a way to encourage natives to assimilate into the majority population—a recurrent theme in federal Indian policy. The result of all this was to reduce the acres of Klamath reservation, established in that 1864 treaty, from 1.9 million acres to 800,000 acres a few decades later.

Whatever the predictions of the government agents, the Klamath natives were not self-sufficient going into the 1900s, many still relying on native foods as well as the food rations from the government. Well, at risk of being facetious, this writer could say that maybe the government itself was partly at fault for this continued dependence, for failing to follow the admonition of the 1864 treaty. As spelled out in the treaty, the dominant whites, of a religious bent, concluded that the natives needed some "civilization" and moral improvement if they were to advance beyond hunting, fishing and, yes, farming. Lacking in civilization and morality? (Two years earlier, a U.S. commissioner of Indian affairs had referred to their "barbarous customs.")

Trulove and Bunting noted in a research paper on the Klamaths that the benefits of this "civilization" would quickly come to mean "short hair, (western) dress and religion as well as instruction in English, foreign customs, and agriculture. In short, the self-sufficient Klamath were intro-

II. Dependent

duced to a new life style which would force them to lose their traditional habits and hurry them toward 'civilization'—a transition which officials estimated would take about twenty years."[17]

Some of the government agents, themselves ordained ministers, would seek to "civilize" the Klamaths (some education would help, too). The arrogance of this commitment is rooted in a belief, expressed decades earlier, that the natives looked upon the whites as superior beings. Scholar Stern observed that it must have been difficult to maintain that estimate in the face of the government's administrative obstinacy, trying, for example, to force the natives to be farmers despite the futility of the effort.

One of the "barbarous customs, as the government agent saw it, was the infliction of capital punishment on tribal members guilty of homicide. (Really, is it still generally viewed as "barbarous" as practiced in many states today?) The response of the government agents to this "barbarity" was to severely punish the perpetrators. Not to be intimidated, the response of a native leader was, "We are not your slaves that you should punish us for executing our own laws…Why do you meddle with our business?" (You could call it an early version of states rights.)[18]

The Indian affairs commissioner who wrote of the barbarous customs did note, however, that the government had signed treaties elsewhere giving the Klamaths the understanding they were a free and independent nation, assuring them that the title of law would apply to their customs, onerous or not. The commissioner, accepting the reality of the situation, favored treating the Klamaths as a colony, helping enforce their laws and providing funds to improve their lives.[19] Their dependency lived on.

This stated desire to "improve the lives" of the native people reflects, by this one government agent, a humane concern for their wellbeing, a concern that goes beyond the branding of the original Americans as barbarous thieves and cowards, as found in the telling commentaries of the Indian-affairs commissioners in the 1880s. Government agent Dyar expressed this humanitarian motivation when he admitted that though attempts to promote farming were unlikely to succeed, "I think it is better to gratify and encourage them by helping them all I can in their efforts at agriculture as in doing so they are acquiring habits of industry and at the same time are preparing themselves to take care of the cattle which they now have and which I hope to see rapidly increase."

The fact is that some Indian affairs officials of the government held a profoundly romantic view— maybe naive is a better word—of the natives, as if they were pure specimens of the human race, to be encouraged to be more like white people, while being protected from the vices of these same white people. J. W. Perit Huntington, superintendent of Indian affairs for Oregon, certainly projected this view when he wrote to a subordinate that his duty was to maintain a strictly Indian settlement, "carefully guarding it against the contamination of white associations, and at the same time imparting to it so much of the intelligence, enterprise and stability of the Anglo Saxon Race as possible."[20] Well, the whites were not all a source of contamination.

(Later, when the reservation was opened up to the harvest of timber, the "white associations" indeed were contaminant. According to one account. "The Klamath had as their model of white behavior the often drunken, lawless, promiscuous antics of loggers and related timber 'beasts.' 'I do not believe,' the agency superintendent reports, 'that the moral condition is much, if any, worse among Indians than it is among the same class of white people on and near the reservation.'"[21] (A little perspective on the human condition is helpful, though one can dispute whether the Klamaths were of the same lowly class as the lawless loggers.)

In those earlier treaty years, most Klamaths no longer subsisted solely on wild game and the food of natural plants. They also received the payments and food rations from the government overlords as compensation for the taking of their land. According to Stern, the Klamaths under treaty could aspire to own a farm and horses or cattle, to dress well as men of substance, to enjoy the coffee, sugar, salt, beef and other new "necessities," as well as to send their children to school. But to achieve these benefits, Stern wrote, they were expected to work hard, subject themselves to an alien discipline, and over time to abandon their native religion in favor of the Christianity of the Methodist church.[22]

II. Dependent

As could be expected, though, the effort to make the Klamaths dependent on an alien religion did not go smoothly, not just because of native resistance, but partly because of friction between church morality and government administration of the reservation. And this passage by the unofficial historian Stern is delicious: "At one point this caused Agent E. L. Applegate to cry—with a measure of histrionic license to be sure—has the United Church in this state established the Inquisition over the Indian service? Should it Interest Congress to know that our branch of the public service be rushed back to the methods of the 15th century?" He was referring, of course, to the vicious, violent attempts by the Roman Catholic church to stamp out, through torture and worse, the heretics of those times. It seems that the Methodist missionaries, from a church born of opposition to the Church of England and now acting on behalf of the American government, accused a government agent of allowing the Indians to dance and hold horse races during Fourth of July celebrations. Not to mention the missionary criticism of the agents, even by the wife of a churchman.[23] Yes, church and state don't mix too well, as we see today as the Catholic church seeks to impose on the body politic—and on its own members—its views on abortion and birth control.

Even then, a Methodist missionary would later side with the natives in their difficult relationship with the government. Ricky D. Gassaway of the Cookson Hills Center of the United Methodist Mission, which serves Cherokee people in Oklahoma, wrote, "Over the last 150 years, the government has tried a series of conflicting ways of dealing with the natives of this continent—making war on them, making treaties with them, breaking treaties with them, sending them to Oklahoma (Modocs, after they lost their war), forcing them onto reservations, forcing them off reservations, permitting them to own land collectively, forcing them to divide the land onto individual plots…outlawing the practice of their religion, legalizing practice of those religions…(and so forth)" The accuracy of some of his assertions is faulty, but the thrust of his claim of the difficult relationship is right on.[24]

Actually, when the government did try to stamp out the native religion of the Klamaths, it used the transplanted Methodist religion to make them

The Dependency Curse

more "civilized" and more amenable to control. The Klamaths brought in lumber to help build a church. And native leaders, as well as government agents, took part in Methodist services, natives being ordained as preachers to extol the benefits of the Christian way. At Sunday school, children were given bibles and prompted to read verses. One of the government preachers was Joseph Emery, the agent who tried to make farmers out of the natives. Now he was making Christians of them, threatening in one sermon to punish them severely if they got into trouble.

Unlike preacher Emery, however, let's not look upon the native people as an inferior "them," different from the white newcomers, needing instruction from the overlords, unable to rise above their dependent status as government wards. Stern observed, "From the first, the Klamath demonstrated an eagerness to turn new opportunities to advantage, coupled with an independence that sometimes strained administrative patience." (Running the lives of others isn't so easy.) For example, when a sawmill was created in 1870 as authorized in the treaty of 1964, they promptly began to cut and haul sawlogs, some used to build native dwellings and others sold to the government and outsiders for a lucrative trade. The natives were not deterred when the U.S. Supreme Court ruled in 1873 that reservation Indians had no authority to cut timber except to clear land for farming. Thus in those early years, government policy sought to prevent the Indians from harvesting and selling their own timber. Many of the natives, including at least three chiefs, took part in the illicit traffic. Whites who bought the lumber stoutly avowed they didn't know it was against the law to do so, Stern said. (More than three decades later Congress finally removed the restriction and allowed payment to tribal members the money made from the sale of their forbidden timber. More on this to come.)

"For the Klamath," he wrote, "their operations in the timber market were more than an exercise in resourcefulness and industry, they provided experience and allies in evading what must have seemed a senseless legal prohibition." They also helped the Klamaths become adept at buying and selling, at managing their own finances. Still partly dependent? Yes. Striving to be independent? Absolutely. As one who has traveled through much of

II. Dependent

the world, I can say without equivocation that most people want to make it on their own, except when their governments hold them back or encourage them to be dependent.

On their part, the Klamaths were taking advantage of job opportunities, some with the government as well outside it. It was a showing of the desire to be independent. A tribal account of their lives in the late 1800s noted that many were employed at the government's Indian agency, a military post and in a nearby town, taking such jobs as government police and laborers, and as farmhands for private citizens. A limited number did go into farming and ranching, while others worked on the tribal freighting teams that hauled supplies to meet area needs. (They showed up in 40 horse-drawn wagons at one town to haul provisions for the reservation.) Former chairman Mitchell's mother had a ranch and his father worked on fire towers and guard stations for the U.S. Bureau of Indian Affairs.

How generous of the government to provide jobs? Well, not entirely. In the early years, one government superintendent required the natives to work four days a week on reservation roads before they could get a pass to leave for outside employment. Government agents even used food rations at times as a weapon in an effort to keep the Klamaths on the reservation (stay, or get no food). The Modocs said "go to hell" when deprived of food rations, and left to start a rebellion.

These heavy-handed efforts to "control" the Klamath tribes were not entirely descriptive of the government-native relationship in the first half-century following the creation of the reservation system. Government rule, in fact, was uneven and inconsistent. While the agents punished tribal doctors for practicing spiritual medicine, they deferred to the hereditary chiefs in allowing them to maintain slavery for four years after it was abolished in the nation (so much for the romantic view of native life). The government also permitted the natives to impose tribal justice in their court system, which was sometimes extremely lenient on capital crimes. A father, for example, was fined $50 for killing his child, at least that's what Stern reported. But the overlords worked to establish a democratic system for the election of native leaders, to push aside the recalcitrant hereditary chiefs. In

The Dependency Curse

replacing them, the government relied increasingly on newly elected "progressive" leaders who were used to working with whites and who cooperated with the government, for which they sometimes received appropriate perks.

Looking back on that period, we can see that that Klamaths in some ways became more independent rather than dependent under government dominion. Ironically, the government's failure to fulfill some of its promises to aid the natives caused them to strike out to make money on their own. And the creation of a native police force, with government involvement, to help maintain l (white) law and order, foundered on lack of federal funding, thus freeing the natives of excessive government domination. Nevertheless, the government agents had direct control of the diminished police force and used the cops to their advantage, while bypassing the Indian courts, which were more independent seats of power.

One thing for sure, the Klamaths, already a mixture of more than one tribe, were becoming even more culturally diluted through inter-tribal and native-white sexual relationships. Native women, in particular, were hooking up with white men, in common-law and traditional marriage.[25] (A Modoc woman, Winema, tried to stop the rebellion against government forces.) They also were becoming more tied in to the dominant white culture, moving back and forth to outside jobs and returning periodically to their reservation homes. Those are trends that continue today, just as I found on a journalistic assignment to South Africa, where intermarriage and a common religion were wiping out tribal differences and distinctions.

In a way, the U.S. government was nation-building in that earlier Klamath era, trying to create an "independent," democratic native nation, hoping to make them self-sustaining within a few decades. And make them more peacefully "civilized," or "more like us" as dominant people are wont to do. The arrogance of this effort can be seen in the words of agent Dyer in his rationale for taking children from their homes and educating them in boarding schools on the reservation:

"Being fully convinced that a radical change in the Indian character can only be wrought in childhood and early youth. I would…urge the cooperation of the government in the prosecution of this work of taking the children

II. Dependent

from their native haunts of degradation, and clothing, feeding, and teaching them the habits and arts of civilization."

Whatever the rationale, the schools were of benefit in developing young people to function in outside society, teaching English and other academic subjects as well as vocational skills, even inadvertently helping them learn to circumvent authority (in this case, their teachers). To learn to challenge authority is to learn to function as adults, as we all know. By the same token, in "allowing" the natives to work for whites outside the reservation, the government was planting more seeds of independence. And as that independence grew, crime and a saloon trade grew apace. Let's not forget, now, that the ultimate goal of the government was to create independent nations. It was happening, whether by calculation or not.

So the question must be asked: Was the government any more successful at transforming the Indian society into a viable "modern" nation, than it has been most recently in resolving the tribal and religious conflicts in the "modern" nations of Iraq and Afghanistan? Well, not exactly. In some ways, the government was encouraging the natives to break away from traditional family and community constraints and be more individualistic in the mode of the "white culture." But in prompting the natives to be more like the individualistic whites, the government and its Methodist cohorts made the Klamaths harder to control—more independent. So, lo the poor whites, they were faced with an impossible task, on the one hand and on the other.

The outcome of this government effort, as applied to the Klamaths, should come as no surprise when you consider its component parts: to subjugate, control, patronize, pacify, civilize, Christianize, educate and transform the native people, who often didn't agree with each other, let alone with what the government was trying to do to them and for them. But the effort, however incompatible some of its parts, was not a total failure. Education and English language training helped make a difference. And heredity leaders like the Kirks, became more and more assertive, making many trips to Washington to challenge decisions and hiring attorneys to represent them. Then, soon after the turn of the century, the government in effect gave up and took the easy way out, making them dependent, not on the government, but on unearned money.

CHAPTER III

Independent?

ALL THE EFFORT OF NATION-BUILDING, if it can be called that, came to naught when by an act of Congress the government in essence made the Klamaths a dependent people, and even more dependent in the way it carried out the law.

On June 25, 1910, almost half a century after the Klamaths had been forced to live on a reservation, Congress allowed them to make money from the sale of their timber, an asset of great value, consisting of one of the finest stands of Ponderosa pine in the world.[1]. Eventually a native family of five would receive $4,000 a year, a goodly sum at the time for people who paid no taxes and did nothing to maintain and sell the timber. Close to half came to rely totally on those payments.[2] From that income, the Klamaths were almost self-sufficient, relying little on government assistance. That was a good thing, right? But in an ultimate form of paternalism, Bureau of Indian Affairs (BIA) foresters managed the resource on their own rather than train the natives to take over the management of their property so they could gain job skills, develop a sense of self-worth and become self-reliant. It was the start of a dependency on unearned income that their chairman Seldon Kirk would later lament as such a deleterious benefit.

In a devastating criticism of that dependency, economist Trulove, who had done extensive research on the Klamaths, wrote that the BIA, by shifting control and responsibility from Indians to itself in an attempt to benefit and protect its wards, inadvertently set into motion programs detrimental to its own long-run goals by making Indians increasingly dependent.[3] "Unwilling to devise long-range economic and social development programs using tribal incomes," Trulove said, "the BIA capitulated to Klamath demands and distributed tribal monies per capita in equal shares to all members of the tribe." The natives wanted money, not programs—an understandable motivation. Because of the payments, however, Trulove said the Klamaths had "little incentive to undertake the rigors of education and training or to seek regular employment, living under the illusion of a minimally adequate guaranteed income for life." His research paper was titled, "The economics of paternalism." Dr. Calvin Hunt, a Klamath Falls physician with a large Indian clientele, was more direct, writing that the Klamaths were "a sovereign nation on the dole." Consider that the government, in providing free medical care for the Klamaths, paid Hunt for his services. (Is that biting the hand that fed him?)[4]

As noted above, as a longtime insider, tribal chairman Kirk had seen the negative impact of the per capita payments. As academic outsiders, Trulove and his colleague David Bunting found, in their research, additional problems from the payments: young people were less inclined to get an education or jobs when they were assured an income for life, leading to loss of parental control and high rates of juvenile delinquency; Natives incurred large debts by borrowing against the shares of their children and future timber-sale income; no money from the per capita pool was set aside for economic or social-welfare activities of benefit to the entire tribe.[5]

For the Klamaths, this was the beginning of a dependence that continued for almost half a century, to be replaced by the one-shot fortune they received from the government takeover of their timber, followed by their independence for more than three decades, and, finally, by the restoration, as they insisted, of their dependence on government. Meantime, the Mdewakanton Sioux in Minnesota depended on the government for two decades after they were given tribal status in 1969, to be replaced by their dependence on the fabulous fortune of their gambling casino.

III. Independent?

But some natives are now questioning this dependence, especially for a few tribes, the hundreds of millions of dollars in gambling profits. These critics, scholars and journalists, go beyond just blaming white America for their problems. They look for causes within their own populations as they seek a way out of a long-lasting social and economic depression.

Native reliance on government is the most pervasive of all, the government providing even free health-care coverage as well as employment, education, social services and other benefits. Beyond that, the government frees tribal members from paying any taxes if they live on a reservation (but not in cities). The dependence on gambling is much more limited; less than half the tribes sponsor casinos, and of those that do, only a relatively small number make big profits to share with members. But more and more tribes (now more than half of those with casinos) are providing this "free" money to members, from small to large amounts.

Charles Trimble, a member of the Oglala Lakota Sioux nation of South Dakota, expresses concern over dependence on both government and gambling. The new casino wealth, he says, has improved the lives of natives and helped preserve their culture. But it also brings a new dependency replacing the reliance on a federal largesse that has "eroded families and entire societies among some tribal communities." More specifically, he worries about the effect of gambling money on native young people, comparing them to the nonworking, oil-rich youth in Saudi Arabia who have little purpose in life, some even turning to terrorism.[6] He's not claiming that native youth might go that far, but one actually went pretty far in a horrific killing spree. A while back, a popular young Tulalip Indian in Washington state shot five five other tribal members and killed four of them, along with himself. That case may not relate to Trimble's concerns because Tulalip gambling payments to tribal members probably are too modest to create the empty lives of Saudi youth, and the motive of killer Taylen Fryberg could have been simply that one of his victims had spurned him in a request for a date, which is unlikely. But it is worth mentioning in the search for motives in so many mass killings by young people today, this being the first by a native youth, and thus raising the question of whether dependency and lack of self-worth were factors.[7]

The Dependency Curse

(This author knows first-hand about the idle youth of Saudi Arabia, having traveled there on a reporting assignment for his newspaper.)

Trimble also describes what he sees as the negative impact of the government dependency, how families and their communities rely totally on federal relief programs, how government thus supplants the family, how men are unemployed for years. "A man who has no role in providing for the family has little purpose as a father. He brings nothing to the household, and gradually loses respect from his spouse and children. Thus alienated he will likely resort to alcohol or drugs, leading to despair and early death." Trimble speaks with authority. He is past executive director of the National Congress of American Indians and principal founder of the American Indian Press Association.

Other natives echo the concerns over dependence on government. The president of the National Congress of American Indians, Ed Driving Hawk, observed that tribal governments had become more administrators of federal programs than tribal governments. Prominent native author Vine Deloria Jr. contended that an outpouring of federal aid had created a state of benign confusion, in which Indians seem more concerned with funding programs than with developing more comprehensive ideologies and theories that are necessary for sustained growth.[8] As critics of this dependency see it, gambling revenue can add to the problem, depending on how it is used. The Native Nations Institute for Leadership, Management and Policy, based at the University of Arizona, noted the common argument that the problem arises when tribes pay the money (per capita) to individual natives rather than use it for programs of benefit to the tribal communities as a whole. "Per capita distributions replace one form of individual and family welfare (dependency on federal transfers of funds) with another (dependency on tribal payments). It is still welfare and it has the same effects: reduced interest in education, stagnant or reduced employment, a declining work ethic, growing social problems, a belief that the (tribal) nation should solve all its citizens' problems."[9]

When citizens of one northwestern tribal nation increased its per capita payments, the institute wrote, it threatened cost-of-living adjustments for

III. Independent?

tribal employees, construction of a tribal school and museum, and tribal youth programs. Moreover, said the institute, such a diversion of a significant portion of profits threatens the survival of business enterprises, which rely on the tribes as their primary funding source.

If casino money saps initiative, it also can create a gambling addiction that is even worse. Veteran journalist Tim Giago, also of the Oglala Lakota Sioux nation, an award-winning columnist, founder of four native newspapers, writes, under the headline, "A new addiction is sweeping Indian Country." The addiction to gambling, he says, "has not caused the big splash in Indian country yet, but that splash is coming. If you doubt me just visit any Indian casino on any Indian reservation in this country and you will see many tribal members ensconced at the gaming tables and slot machines in their own casinos. This gambling is already contributing to many new social problems in Indian country. Adults are spending their per capita payments, and their welfare and paychecks at the gaming tables. They are losing money they should have used to buy school clothes for their children, to pay their rent or mortgage or to buy food, some even leaving their children home alone while they feed their gambling addiction at their reservation casinos." Giago could have been saying that many natives already have a terrible addiction to alcohol, and they don't need another one, to gambling.[10]

None of these problems has deterred many native nations from responding to the lure of big amounts of easy money, often sharing it with members to create the new dependence. One nation, the Navaho, held back for a few years, figuring it caused social problems, but overcame its fears and succumbed to the gaming craze, building four—yes, four—casinos on its vast reservation, one a palace along the Interstate 40 freeway. When opening the $230 million Twin Arrows casino-hotel in Arizona, Navaho President Ben Shelly pulled no punches about its purpose in saying, "This place is to make money." None of it will go in per capita payments to members, not because that would be deleterious to their self-worth, but because "there's too many of us" (200,000 or more) to share the wealth—$30 million a year to the tribe. While individual Navaho people have not received part of the money, a news headline pointed out the other side of the story: "Navaho nation economic growth creating jobs and true independence."[11]

Lance Morgan, chief executive of the Ho-Chunk corporation, the economic development arm of the Winnebego tribe of the Upper Midwest, shared the key concern about Indian gaming: those unearned payments to members. "Tribal economics and lifestyles built on per capita payments have almost no chance of long-term sustainability," he said. "This new form of welfare is just the latest in a cycle of dependency that Indian Country has been trying to break out of for over 100 years." But he and other Winnebago leaders were not enough concerned to eschew the establishment of six Winnebago casinos in Wisconsin, to expand four of them and seek two more, in Iowa and Nebraska. Nor enough concerned to keep from making those onerous per capita payments, $48,000 per household each year. Of course, there is more to it than that: Gambling money pulled the tribe out of serious poverty and provides jobs for the tribal members, though, typically for many tribes, less than a third of those jobs are held by Winnebago people.[12]

The tribe suffered a temporary setback when the Nebraska Supreme Court ruled against the proposed casino in that state, where, according to the local newspaper, "Opponents said the social consequences of expanding gambling far outweighed any gains and feared the machines (slots) could be the first step down a slippery slope of social decay." Will Morgan give up? No way. "If anybody knows anything about us," he said, "we're resilient and we're focused, and we'll be back to try it again."[13]

Social decay? When you travel on the freeways around the country, as my wife and I often do, you can see that many tribes don't buy that argument. On some freeways you see what is a spread-out version of Las Vegas, with accompanying billboards, one after another, to advertise the slots to the passing public. Native America has gone public in a big way.

Not all the native gambling, however, is generated by natives themselves. As you might expect, gaming developers are more than happy to "encourage" the expansion, to the benefit of the white developers, of course. Consider the situation at the tiny Timbisha Shoshone community in Death Valley, California. Upon leaving a Death Valley resort after a short stay, my

III. Independent?

spouse and I saw this little "town," home of 50 people, too small for any significant economic development, obviously dependent on government support. When I read about the Shoshone later, I learned that the natives there had rejected sponsoring a casino, but three outside gambling operators supported a rival tribal faction living elsewhere, "supported" them with hundreds of thousands of dollars in cash, free cars, trips and other inducements, according to allegations by the Death Valley community. With that support, the Shoshone outsiders acted to take over control of the Death Valley faction and thereby to sponsor a casino on Shoshone property in a town 100 miles away. As of this writing the casino hasn't happened, the property inhabited by field mice. So help me, that's what it said in the local newspaper. (The losing Shoshone faction obviously didn't have the political clout of the world-giant Genting Group, which won approval for a casino in New York with the aid of a small army of lobbyists and public relations personnel, as well as a well–placed political contribution, as reported in the *New York Times*.).

One of the concerns, meantime, is whether the great potential in Indian gambling will last, as more and more tribal and commercial casinos are established, vying for the same gaming dollar. Native gambling revenue already is growing more slowly than profits of commercial casinos (nationally, 2 percent for Indian casinos on a still-impressive revenue of $28 billion, or half the 4 percent for commercial). So the question is, will the Indian casinos go the way of the buffalo, which sustained the natives for many decades in the American plains? That dependence was ended when white hunters slaughtered millions of the animals to sell their hides—5 million killed in two years.

Surprisingly, writes S. C. Gwynne in his best-selling book on the Comanches, "only a few voices cried out against the slaughter of the buffalo, which had no precedent in human history." On the contrary, says Gwynne, Indian-fighter General Phil Sheridan declared that depriving the Indians of their food supply did more in two years to settle the "vexed" Indian question than the entire regular army had done in 30 years. Starve them into submission, was the implication, but you could argue that eliminating their dependence on the buffalo made them more dependent on the government.[14]

Of course, you can't attribute dependency to all the 5.2 million natives of differing cultures in the 560 tribes scattered across the county. Of that number, barely more than one-third any longer live on reservations, the rest having migrated to cities and towns and living mostly on their own. For those still on the reservations, claims of dependency as a major cause of their social problems can't be proved conclusively, though many native leaders and outside experts, as well as this writer, believe that is the case. (And that's the thesis of this book.) Native author Gerald Vizenor contends that notions of dependency are complicated and demand a close analysis of how changes in federal policies have affected the status of American Indians. Vizenor, professor emeritus of American Studies at the University of California, Berkeley, also objects to an emphasis on "victimry," or on natives as victims, rather than on their survival over the centuries.[15] As we note below, changes in federal policies certainly have affected the dependency or lack of dependency of the Klamath natives.

Looking back at the Klamaths, the amount of money they received monthly from timber sales starting in 1913 seems small compared with today's incomes, but by 1950 the $800 per capita payments enabled a Klamath family of four to exceed the median income for all families in the country, according to Stern. In short, they were not poor. Beyond that, as we have noted, many natives gained a one-time bonus from the sale or lease of their land and for many, an additional supply of food from hunting and fishing. As could be expected, the debilitating effect of a self-imposed lack of work experience put the Klamaths at a big disadvantage if they wanted to be hired at well-paying jobs in the broader community. Most didn't, or couldn't.[16]

The BIA, meantime, didn't exactly distinguish itself at first in managing the Klamath timber, for members of the Klamath tribes. The agency noted later that its policy of achieving high sales prices through vigorous competition for Klamath stumpage was good as far as the Indians' short-term money requirements were concerned. But as demand for the timber increased by "leaps and bounds," high sales prices caused partly by speculators

III. Independent?

threatened the survival of the job-producing sawmill industry and damaged future prospects for the Klamath Indians. "The unregulated depletion of Klamath Indian reservation forest resources would cause the future poverty and dependency of the Indians," the BIA admitted.[17]

Some of the Klamaths were not too concerned about future dependency. In 1915, five years after the sales were approved by Congress, a petition signed by 270 natives—then about a quarter of their population—asked the government to sell and dispose of all the tribal timber lands for cash or reasonable deferred payments. (Forget the lumber mill provided by treaty.) Two years later, the government noted several "indications" from tribal records that the Indians were more interested in selling timber than in incorporating it into a processing business.[18] (The Klamaths were not of one mind, however, on the use of their forest. Some wanted timber income to be used for industrial development, but a loan for that purpose was soon dissipated.)[19]

To its credit, the BIA later adopted a policy designed to protect the timber resource, for the short-term benefit of the local lumber industry and the long-term interest of the Indians. The remedy was to limit the annual cut of Klamath timber to the amount of overall growth of the forest that would replace the trees to be harvested, putting the harvest on a sustained yield basis. The agency concluded that the continued welfare of the Klamaths could best be served through this conservative development of their resources, with an annual timber harvest that would produce an income of about $1 million.

To its discredit, however, the agency's stated rationale for the policy change referred to the natives as though they were children. Rapid liquidation of the Klamath's forest resources, the BIA noted, would "eventually prove fruitfully productive of a worthless people, wholly dependent upon the mercy of the government for life and sustenance. Experience has conclusively demonstrated that it is by far the safer and easier policy to conserve tree capital than to prevent the Indian from dissipating funds received through the liquidation of this asset."[20]

So, by managing the Klamath forest on a sustained yield basis, the government made it possible to pay the natives each year, starting at $500 and then up to that $800 per member. The irony is that this policy, while it avoided making the Klamaths wholly dependent on the mercy of the government, made them dependent on the unearned per capita payments. The per capita payments were reduced during the depression of the 1930s, forcing more natives to find work. (Many already had been working to supplement their per capita payments.) The dependency could have been averted if at least part of the money had been used for economic development and forest-management training of the natives for the long range. As we have seen, however, a large number of the Indians wanted the money for their private use, not for development and training. (Trulove contends, however, that it is unrealistic to expect much economic development in rural areas, such as the Klamath reservation, because markets, trained labor forces and other inputs "are simply not there and never will be.")[21]

It is worth noting, however, that the Klamaths were not passively dependent while receiving the "free money" from timber sales or the lump sum payment upon sale of the entire forest under termination.

They aggressively sought tens of millions of dollars from the government as compensation for the taking and management of their land. And they were willing to accept, as a ploy, the white government's description of them as an "ignorant and uneducated" people at the time they signed the treaty of 1864, being unaware of what they were entitled to receive for their land, acting under the "dominance and influence of the government agents."[22] These "ignorant and uneducated" people did pretty well in raking in additional millions of dollars.

In one case the Klamaths sought $90 million for the government's alleged mismanagement of their forest, and finally settled for $16 million—a considerable sum. In all, they were awarded more than $30 million over a period of years in their claims for additional compensation.[23] The government was hardly penurious in making these awards. The $16 million, for example, was based on what could be called a dubious claim of forest mismanagement, when the government in fact established a sustained yield policy to protect the forest from an over-cutting that would be to the

III. Independent?

detriment of the Klamaths in the long run, as this writer pointed out above.

Their continued dependency on government money was ended, however, when Congress decided in the late 1950s to disband the Klamath tribe (as well as a small number of other tribes) and pay members for their timber assets. Congress had begun to consider the plan in hearings a decade earlier, prompting Klamath chairman Seldon Kirk and his father Jesse Kirk, also a tribal official, to write to the Klamath superintendent about what they called an "abominable" scheme to deprive the natives "of everything they hold dear and everything they possess."

"Never in all the history of the Indian race," they wrote, "has such a blatantly foul scheme to cheat and rob its members been evolved. So monstrous is it, in fact, as to be increditable; and our first reaction was to disregard it as being too crassly infamous, as well as stupid, to be worth bothering about. But imbecile as the document may appear, as vicious and incredible, as it sounds, it is being taken seriously by those sponsoring it, and being pressed. Nor can we remain blind to the fact that many times before, many, many times, the Indians of America have been cheated, swindled and robbed by methods, just as flagrantly cold-blooded, just as merciless, just as cruel, and just as stupid and unbelievable as those outlined in the document we submit, that is a matter of history and cannot be ignored."[24]

The letter obviously relies on a bit of exaggeration to make their case, in view of the fact that the government was proposing to pay the Klamaths for their timber, rather than rob them. But it makes an essential point in a PS: "The attached bill says that tribal members are 'demanding their independence.' This is not true; the Klamath tribes have not as yet asked for this. This statement is made on the proposed bill purely to mislead." Kirk obviously did not feel the tribe was ready for independence at that time.

And therein lies the ambiguity of the Klamaths on dependence versus independence while in the reservation system, partly because of the misdirection and failures of government policies, partly by their own choices. In the chronology this author is developing, the government first tried to make the Klamaths independent by forcing them into farming on land unsuitable for growing crops. Then the government encouraged them to go into ranch-

The Dependency Curse

ing but they lost much of their initiative and sold most of their cattle when they were allowed to depend on revenue from timber sales. The Klamaths understandably chose to take the money, without demanding the training, nor was it offered by the government, by which they could have taken over management of their forest resource. Besides all that, they were permitted to sell or lease their land to whites, and many did. (By 1927 one white rancher had acquired 7,000 acres of Klamath land.)[25] That's what happened during the reservation years. Finally, in the decision that drew the ire of the Kirks, the government decided to terminate the reservation and pay off the Klamath for their resources. At last, the Klamaths were mostly independent, on their own, but unhappily so, and after three decades they won back their tribal status and their dependence. More on this below.

Meantime, going back to the reservation years for context, Indian superintendent L. D. Arnold wrote in 1926: I do not believe that there are one thousand head of cattle owned by Indians on the reservation at the present time. Last year the most prominent Indian stockman sold almost his entire herd for about $35,000—the last of the Indians who were formerly prosperous." (Actually, there were prosperous native ranchers way beyond that time.)

And there was another benefit for the Klamaths in the timber-sale money. Stern noted that "having money gave at least partial emancipation from (government) agency surveillance.[26]

Stern summarized the state of the Klamaths thusly: "In the limbo into which reservation society was thrust, its constituent units (presumably family and tribal government) continued to erode; and the administration, which had planned to transform them, now found them so weakened that it had to bear the major task of regulating the conduct of tribal members. Tribal members, finding that the chief restraint upon their conduct was wielded by the agency, increasingly rebelled."

And rebel they did. The women rebelled in forming common-law relationships with white men, since they were not allowed to marry them—Oregon did not repeal this prohibition until 1951. The men and women also rebelled in making, buying, selling and drinking liquor, another draconian

III. Independent?

ban not eliminated until 1951. Think of it, these original Americans had to wait until the early 1950s to be granted certain rights other Americans had long taken for granted. (Actually, the U. S. Supreme Court didn't over-rule interracial marriage until 1967, though it had already been approved by many states, like Oregon). Not only that, as we have observed, the natives had not been granted citizenship until 1924, some thousands of years after they had settled in this vast land.[27]

The Klamaths, however, had a weapon to avert outright white oppression and discrimination. They could reject white contracts for the sale of their priceless timber, which provided a major part of the economies of the surrounding dominant white population.

So this grand experiment in a paternalistic government control over the natives had produced mixed results for the Klamaths and the white government. For the government, maintaining control over the native "ghetto" dwellers was difficult. For the native people, life was much easier in depending on the sale of their timber for annual payments.

The easier life, however, was not preferred by many of the Klamaths, such as Barbara Alatorre. Like half the Klamaths, Alatorre and her family lived independently away from their reservation in earlier years, not dependent on the federal government. Along with other Klamaths, her parents went north in the 1950s to work— in canneries and berry fields—because there were few jobs on the reservation. In Portland, daughter Barbara later worked on programs for other natives, went through three husbands, raised seven children, enrolled in community college so she could write better in her volunteer job of tribal historian. Now, at age 70, suffering from the constant pain of spinal problems, she navigates her home in an electric wheelchair, still radiating strength and resolve, still pushing to regain their reservation and land. She's an organizer, leader, researcher, speaker, critical thinker: soft-spoken in conversation, outspoken against "cheaters and crooks" in government—and in her tribal leadership.[28]

Phil Tupper, during his 73 years, didn't opt for the easier life either. He managed the family ranches of 6,000 acres, largest combined land holding on the reservation. He also was a rodeo performer, eventually becoming a national college champion. But rather than go on the national rodeo circuit, he chose to remain home with his wife and children. Tupper described his earlier and later life in an interview with author Roberta Ulrich, how he loved horses ("I always wanted to be a cowboy; everything I ever did was on horseback"), went everywhere by horse, not car; was raised to be tough, not like the young people who he says die early or go to jail because of drugs and alcohol, how he loved the beauty of his family's ranch with the many horses and cattle and two barns built with hand-hewed wood pegs, how he and his wife raised six children and a grandson in 55 years of marriage, how two of his sons in the family tradition of work got jobs in the Klamath lumber mill. And how he learned about ranching from his grandfather, a traditionalist, who "prayed every night in Indian language after it got dark. (It was) another world."[29]

As you can see, the Alatorre and Tupper families functioned independently on the basis of self-interest. As did their tribe. But the self-interest of the tribe was based more on dependence than on independence. Certainly it was self-interest that caused the Klamaths to push for increased timber sales earlier in the last century to boost payments to members,[30] and then, when they no longer owned the timber, to oppose sales as a claimed threat to their hunting and fishing rights, especially as related to mule deer.[31]

On a national level, for all the romantic talk of native devotion to nature and the land, it was self-interest that prompted early tribal people, in order to survive, to wipe out vegetation where they lived in the arid southwest, and then to move on to other areas where they would do the same. It was self-interest for Indians to slaughter buffalo for their tongues, which they considered a delicacy. It also was self-interest that led the Ojibway to fight the Sioux for territory in the northern plains, before the intrusion of white settlers. And, finally, it was self-interest that prompted the Europeans to push out the natives to clear the way for farmers, miners and other newcomers. It amounted to the building of an empire, much as the Comanches and the Sioux had earlier built their empires.

But the original inhabitants, in this case the Klamaths, did not share equally in the benefits of that white man's empire. Sure, the children were

III. Independent?

now being educated and the adults were enjoying many of the same material goods as their white overlords. Still, as dependents, they were not equal. The late chairman Seldon Kirk, as quoted earlier this account, lamented the second-class status of his Klamath people. He would put it in a different way in this statement to his council: "When the white men made a treaty with the Klamath in 1864, they said, 'In twenty years you will be just like white men, no difference.' But when twenty years went by, no white men. And they said, 'Twenty years more.' After that time still no white men. It is now nearly ninety years, and I ask you, 'When will we be like white men?'"[32]

A decade earlier, in 1944, a government man said the Klamaths in some ways already had achieved that status. By then, the white superintendent in charge of their reservation concluded that they were as well off as the whites, finally, close to a century after their reservation was established. Think of it, as he did, the natives dress and live like their white neighbors, are even proficient in English. (Isn't that just amazing?) Their homes are modern, most with electricity, waterworks and sewer systems, and equipped with modern labor-saving devices. They also own many tractors, trucks and other farm and ranch equipment, as well as the better grade of livestock. In fact, as Supt. B. G. Courtright saw it, "The Klamaths already live and have been living, generally speaking, in the same manner and, in many respects, better than their white neighbors. They are much advanced over many other tribes of Indians in the United States."[33]

How did this happen? The timber development program, said Courtright, raised their standard of living to a par of their white neighbors, gave them an opportunity to work in the woods and mills, and made it possible for them to increase their livestock holdings and farming equipment, to a point they could make an adequate living from ranching and farming. The fact is, however, most Klamaths did not take advantage of those opportunities; with guaranteed timber income, they didn't have to go to work. Instead of ranching, they were "promiscuously" and "recklessly" selling off their livestock and their land, according to the Klamaths themselves. See below for more detail on these sales.[34]

Tribal leader Kirk knew the sad truth. He knew that many of the

The Dependency Curse

Klamaths had not achieved the same standard of living as their white neighbors, having been coddled by the unearned income from timber sales, and having lost their initiative. He described their rundown housing as an example of their living conditions and wondered when they would achieve equality with those white people. The government man probably was telling his bosses in Washington what they wanted to hear when he said they already had done so.

The Klamaths, said the government man, were doing so well very few of them any longer relied on their treasured hunting and fishing rights for their subsistence. "Deer are plentiful, but probably only five or six Indians make any profit from deer hides," he said. And "possibly not more than 50 families do any real fishing for subsistence purposes. Fish, some years ago, was the principal source of food, especially at the time of signing of the treaty in 1864."[35]

Supt. Courtright also must have pleased his bosses when he noted that the Klamaths were almost self-sufficient, not counting on taxpayers for support. In two decades up to that time, the natives had received $10 million from timber sales. As a result, they relied not at all on the government for welfare relief, health-care services or aid to the old, infirm, blind and indigent. Speaking for the Klamaths, government boss Courtright wrote in his report that they were content with their situation (he could have said, "with their lot"). Further, they showed no desire to regain any of the land they had lost to the government; instead, Courtright said, "almost all of the tribe" wanted to liquidate the forest" for the immediate proceeds, having voted against land acquisition several times. (As we will note below, the Klamaths were already selling off part of their reservation to whites.)[36]

The government man's assertion in 1944 that "almost all" of the tribe wanted to sell off their forest was probably an exaggeration, calculated to pave the way for termination (an opinion of the author). A government witness in another legal action said later that there were "several indications" in tribal records that there was more interest in selling timber, for payments to tribal members, than incorporating it in a processing business. "Several indications" is not the same as "almost all."

III. Independent?

While touting the self-sufficiency of the Klamaths, the government admitted they endured some deficiencies, such as the need for more and better health assistance as well as improved high-school completion rates. And "too much" of the land available for cattle ranching was leased to non-Indian outsiders. So Courtright laid out a plan to improve their lot, again relying mostly on tribal funds from the timber sales. His detailed, 48-page assessment of assets and needs called primarily for an increase in cattle ranching to compensate for an eventual decline in timber-sale income. That would require such things as fencing and water development for the ranches as well as control of coyotes that were becoming a menace to the livestock industry. "Beyond a doubt," he wrote, "the economy of this reservation is one of raising cattle with sufficient farm lands to produce such foods as can be raised for human consumption and to produce the necessary feeds for winter feeding of livestock."[37]

The Courtright report makes it clear that for all the economic and "civilizing" improvements of the Klamaths, the government had no illusions that there would be a quick fix on the "deep-rooted ills" of native people, as described in an earlier government report (now we are told that the natives were not so well off after all). Now the government agents were no longer talking about 20-year plans for the Klamaths. Instead, as proposed by the natives themselves, they called for long-range programs to deal with those long-time problems.

The Klamaths had no illusions either about their status or needs. As they described it in their 8-page report, presented at the tail end of the 48-page Courtright document, they conceded the obvious: That it would take time to escape their continued dependency on the government. This is worth quoting in full: "The Klamath tribes are not unmindful of the facts that a great deal of time will have been consumed ere (before) the goal of self-government is reached and to undo what much more than a generation has instilled in the minds of our present generation, a something that might be described a feeling of so-called 'dependency' or as something which was never intended as is realized now.

Continuing: "However, now that that the seed has been sown the harmful weeds must be extracted ere (before) the harvest. In order that a good crop be reaped the guiding hand of the Indian Service, we think, must continue, not in accordance with a timetable, but with the flow of accomplishments that will lead us eventually to real citizenship and real self-government, with standards and the same economy as those of our white brothers. As each accomplishment is attained so will the government's trusteeship be diminished that much more quickly. "

And this is the most telling point: "It took the government eighty years to bring us to where we are today—eighty years, many of them, bringing with them wrongs, wrongs not of our making and which cannot be righted in a day, a year, or twenty years."

No, the Klamaths did not agree with the government that by the mid-1940s they were living as well as or better than their white neighbors. Nor did they agree, moreover, that they owed their civilized life largely to the government's decision allowing them to get the benefit of the sales of their timber. Rather, they took credit for how they moved beyond their primitive state. This commentary also is worth quoting in full: "During the early stages of the transition from primitive Indian life to that of a civilized existence; from endeavors to sustain life by means of edible roots, fish, berries and wild animal life, plentiful over a wide domain, to the very much narrowed-down means afforded by the Klamath Indian Reservation, the tribes had one advantage: They knew, from the experience derived from generations who had to support themselves entirely by their own efforts, however primitive their methods may have been, that if one would live, one must provide the wherewithal. Thus meagerly endowed, and without education of any kind, the tribes slowly evolved, diffusing their knowledge among their members, and gradually leading their generations to civilization."

As the Klamaths described their evolution, they went from the "narrowed down means" afforded by their reservation, to the millions of dollars they received in the per capita payments from the timber sales. These payments, as we have noted, made it possible for families to maintain a reasonable standard of living, and for the tribe to pay for basic services,

III. Independent?

without aid from the government. Most of the Klamaths relied solely on those payments, or on additional income from low-wage jobs.[38]

As tribal leader Kirk noted so tellingly, however, the Klamaths were not as well off as the whites. Why not? The tribe conceded that the unearned income "had its ill effects in that it destroyed the incentive to work." This meant that some didn't see the need to get jobs or go into ranching to supplement their "free money." Instead, Kirk said, many of them spent their timber-sale income foolishly. He didn't go into detail on the foolish spending, but the tribe implied that too much of it went into automobiles. ("The advent of the automobile wrought havoc," the tribe said.)

The Klamaths did find another way to supplement their timber-sale payments: sell off their land and cattle. Elaborating on what I wrote above, the tribe itself notes, "Land was sold promiscuously by Indians in their attempt to keep pace with white people and to participate in the new and faster trend of life. Livestock was disposed of as recklessly and for the same reason" (Think of the irony here: The Klamaths rightly complained earlier about the loss of land to white settlers in the 19th century, but then sold 100,000 acres of prime land to other white people in the 20th century, according to their own account.)

Both the Klamaths and the government warned, meantime, that the glory days of "free money" would be diminished in the future: timber harvests would be cut back by as much as half to sustain the resource. The harvest would have to be reduced to maintain virgin timber until new growth was ready for cutting. The harvest already had fluctuated up and down depending on economic conditions.[39]

So how would the tribe make up for the lesser timber income? As did the government, the tribe turned to cattle, proposing to develop irrigation projects to increase native ranching. This would be done under the continued guidance of the government, without any cost to the government. Now wait a minute here. The tribe wanted to boost ranching at the same time they were selling off their cattle for quick cash. It could be described, however, as a sort of panacea, because not all natives would want or be able to raise cattle, and as we have noted, farming was not a viable option.

CHAPTER IV

Terminated

THE PLANS FOR OTHER SOURCES of income came to nothing when the government bought the Klamath forest under an ill-fated termination policy. Termination, as we have noted, meant that the government would pay the Klamaths a large lump sum for their forest, eliminating their monthly income from timber sales. The government must have forgotten that it said three decades earlier that the liquidation of this tribal asset and the end of the monthly payments would create "a worthless people, wholly dependent upon the mercy of the government for life and sustenance." Of course, the government figured that the one-time payment would make the Klamaths a "worthy" people. Tribal leaders like Kirk knew that one-time infusions of money did not solve long-time problems. The Klamaths, they said, were not prepared to deal with sudden wealth. (And how many people are?)

Some congressional advocates of termination saw it as a free-enterprise solution to native dependency, and a less expensive one at that. The leading proponent of the policy, Republican Sen. Arthur Watkins of Utah, believed that people should achieve their goals without government assistance. But not all the support for termination grew out of a conservative philosophy. Consider the opinion of Indian Affairs Commissioner Dillon Myer, who had supervised the internment of American citizens of Japanese ancestry during World War II. He considered those camps as a necessary evil to be done away with as soon as possible. Similarly, he viewed the native reservations as prisons, whose "inmates" were long overdue for freedom.

Scholar Patrick Haynal summarized the status of the Klamaths in the 1950s, when termination was in process: "The decade of the 1950s presents us with a people whose government was subservient to the government of the United States, who were conditioned to economic paternalism instead of self-reliance, who suffered from serious alcoholism, and who had become mistrustful of others, including each other. The federal government had treated the Klamath as children who were allowed to play adult games without any real self-responsibility...The average Klamath in the 1950s was under-educated, lacked economic sophistication, and was not accepted by the dominant society."[1]

Boyd Jackson, Klamath treasurer, told Congress in 1959 that it would take not less than 15 to 20 years before the tribe would be ready to talk about "whether or not we are prepared to go on our own." (Jackson was throwing the government's 20-year plan back in the face of the same government.)

Native author Donald Fixico agrees: "The architects of federal Indian policy failed to realize that assimilating Native Americans into middle-class America would take more time and effort than they wanted to provide. A large portion of the Indian population continually preferred to maintain distinct cultural communities. Furthermore, the existence of minority enclaves in large cities is evidence that Indians and other ethnic groups were not ready to assimilate and white society did not encourage acceptance of Indians."[2]

This author is not sure, however, what is meant by "middle-class America." That amorphous body of people consists of many minorities and ethnic groups, many of whom prefer to associate with their own kind in neighborhoods and churches, while others mix with each other in jobs, social groupings and self-interested support groups. Some Klamaths, like Barbara Alatorre in Portland, get together to advance their causes, but unknown others become isolated, living in urban ghettos and subsisting on alcohol and public or private relief.

IV. Terminated

Yes, some Klamaths, a minority, wanted over the years to shake off the yoke of long-time dependency and cash in their timber resource, those exceedingly valuable Ponderosa pine trees. Others didn't feel that the tribes were ready to be terminated and would squander their sudden wealth, leaving them as an impoverished people, bereft of further government aid or timber-sale payments.

At no time did the Klamaths vote to approve of being terminated. A majority of the tribe opposed it. Congress decided on its own that it would be best for them to assimilate into the white European culture, despite the objections of tribal leaders. At that point, the tribe was given one choice: whether to take the money from the sale of their reservation, or not. In that vote, an overwhelming 78 percent of the three tribes that make up the Klamath nation voted for the money (surprise!); the 22 percent minority decided to keep their part of the reservation, to be managed by trustees. Some of those who decided to leave were so anxious to get their cash they pledged their payments, two years before they were doled out, to buy and resell fringe units of the reservation. Some resold their newly acquired timber and land at a considerable loss, less than they were worth, but no matter, they got money. Thus their dependency on unearned free money would live on, regardless of how achieved.

That was more than 50 years ago. At that time a reporter from upstate Portland (that would be this author) went down to investigate what was happening at the reservation near Klamath Falls, where he had worked one summer. This is how one of his four reports began:

"Klamath Falls, Aug 24, (1959). A Klamath Indian and his family used to live in a rundown house on a dusty dirt road in a suburb here. An old pickup truck was parked in the driveway. Today that family lives in a neat, well-kept home on a paved street. A new car is out front.

"Another Klamath Indian walked into a Klamath Falls automobile agency, pulled out a $28,000 check and purchased a long, sleek car—one of the most expensive makes. On the way to Portland the auto struck a deer. The Indian left the car alongside the road and bought another new auto in Eugene to finish the trip."

The Dependency Curse

"Each of these tribal members had recently obtained a large bonanza from the resale of fringe area land. The two examples point to a simple fact: You can't generalize about the members of this southern Oregon tribe. Some spend their money foolishly on new cars and alcohol (guess that makes most Americans "foolish"). Others buy homes, land and cattle."

The writer was not perceptive enough early in his journalistic career to pass judgment on how white merchants were ripping off the natives on some of their purchases, such as a nonworking $25 typewriter selling for $111, a refrigerator worth $30 drawing $111, and a water pump valued at $17 going for $115. No question about it, many of the Klamaths, not accustomed to making and handling large amounts of money, were easy prey to rapacious white merchants.

And that was just the beginning, two years before the withdrawing tribal members would receive $43,000 apiece, or more than $215,000 for a family of five. A decade later each native received another $12,000 in a land settlement with the government, bringing the family payment to $275,000. Then came the astounding payout of $600,000 for that family of five in the early 1970s when the remaining tribal members voted to sell off their stake in the reservation. It would take almost 80 years for this reporter to accumulate that much money on his $8,000 annual salary at that time.

In all, that amounted to a $220 million payment to the Klamaths for their timber; no other tribe in the country received so much money when they were terminated. Some Klamaths complained., however, that the government made double that amount from timber sales after it took over their land, though this does not account for the effect of inflation. Some also objected to the loss of guaranteed social services such as health, education and housing, which would be worth up to $148 million in the 25 years they were terminated—a government dependency they felt was owed to them under their treaty long past.

Despite this cash infusion, Klamath leaders later played victimhood to the hilt. In a long account of termination "from the tribe's point of view," the Klamaths contended that the federal action, taken without their approval, was the second time the government victimized them, the first being in 1864

IV. Terminated

when by treaty they gave up most of their territory and were confined to a reservation.[3]

In their account, published in 1999 in the Klamath Falls Herald and News, the Klamaths said that the treaty wiped out their economy and trade and forced them to survive on a subsistence basis on their diminished reservation and "meager" federal services. Later, these "resourceful and productive people...recreated their vigorous economy from timber and livestock, to become one of the wealthiest and strongest" tribes in the country. During that time, the Klamaths wrote, they were a well-integrated people, economically prosperous, politically active, culturally and spiritually vital while on their reserved homelands. Well, that's one version of life on the reservation.

Then came termination, the policy "designed to deliberately destroy their economy and undermine their culture." The "horror" of termination, the Klamaths said, took away their most valuable natural resource—their timber—and inflicted great psychological damage by causing them to be branded as "sell-outs" for agreeing to the cash payout.

Klamaths separately tell of increased social pathology, alcoholism, families falling apart, children winding up in foster care. "We broke apart," said tribal elder Lynn Schonchin.[4] Former chairman Mitchell related how his father went to prison while son Jeff and siblings went into a foster home.[5] (Actually, the Klamaths appear to have carried many of their existing problems with them after they were terminated, shown most strikingly by an average life span of only 43 years a mere decade into termination, hardly enough time for any drastic change in that key health measurement.)[6]

As the Klamaths told it in their tribal account, termination made them the most victimized tribe in America. That account was presented by Allen Foreman, then the tribal chairman, and prepared by "a number of" unidentified writers. This victimization by the federal government, they wrote, was done without any studies about the economic, social or cultural impact of the action. Before termination of their federal status, according to the commentary, "these were a well-integrated people, economically prosperous, politically active, culturally and spiritually vital while on their reserved homeland." Before termination, the Klamaths also said, they "enjoyed a reasonably stable tribal government and relationship with the BIA (Bureau of Indian Affairs) for over three generations." It was an uncharacteristic depiction of the oft-criticized BIA.

Let's be honest, however, about this over-all "lo, the poor Indian" account by the tribe itself. Much of it is more or less self-serving hyperbole based on some questionable claims. A most glaring misstatement is that the Klamaths "recreated" their economy in recent decades, when in fact the economy was restored by the federal decision to pay tribal members from a continuing sale of timber. As for lack of studies, the tribe concedes that a study by the Stanford Research Institute concluded that the termination law was "ill-conceived" and could not be enforced without doing "great harm to the Indians." Moreover, the account notes that the U.S. Department of Interior, patron of the Klamaths, recommended against termination. And most victimized of all? More than the tribes who were forced from their homelands to live far away in alien lands? Hardly. The Klamath tribe retained the core of its homeland, while the two smaller tribes who lived with the Klamaths came from nearby territory. By comparison, the Cherokee people in the early 1800s were forced to march from Georgia to Oklahoma in bitter winter weather, in what was called the Trail of Tears, thousands dying enroute. (Today the Cherokee are considered a great economic success built on thriving business ventures.)

In truth there is also a bit of romanticism in the Klamath tribal account, a romanticism more often found in white depictions of the native people dating back to the time Columbus "discovered" America. The tribal account, for example, portrays the good times early on when the Klamaths lived off the land, but ignores the occasional hunger they endured during drought or extreme cold in a harsh climate, or their description of that life as primitive. The account also claims that the tribe was decimated partly by wars perpetrated by whites, but ignores the tribal raiding parties against rival natives, the taking of slaves to trade for horses and its retaliatory killing of many whites.

The most telling "recreation" of their history is found in the claim, "The

IV. Terminated

Klamaths have never and do not now wish to participate in federal welfare dependency." A recreation of history? Yes, the Klamaths successfully fought to regain federal status in the mid-1980s, making them dependent on federal funding for a host of social and government programs. And the tribe also wanted to rewrite their history, seeking the return of their land as though it was taken from them without their consent, when in fact most of them voted to give up the land in exchange for a large payment, only a minority of them voting to keep their part of the reservation, a decision they later reversed.

Further, the Klamaths said that the federal government tried to force them, under termination, to assimilate into the majority white population, but the tribal account fails to mention that many Klamaths were by their own choice leaving their remote reservation to find jobs in the cities. Oh, and remember that the federal government at first tried to "make" the Klamaths a self-sustaining entity, within 20 years no less. As we have noted, that ill-directed effort was a big failure.

The Klamaths were correct in citing how self-dealing white merchants, unscrupulous white attorneys and even non-Indian spouses ripped off part of the native wealth derived from termination. According to their account, attorneys lent themselves money from native accounts or charged exorbitant fees while white men married Indian women, had them declared incompetent and gained control of their assets, or wasted the women's assets and then left.

The Seattle regional office of the Federal Trade Commission, responding to a report of complaints by the Native American Rights Fund, found that white merchants engaged in discriminatory, deceptive and fraudulent practices to help themselves to the Klamath riches.[7] It was not uncommon, the FTC noted, for the merchants to take advantage of the Klamaths in their purchase of everything from automobiles and land to the providing of credit and vehicle warranties, or even in failing to honor advertized specials. Let's not overlook the attorney who stole $100,000 from the estates of two Klamaths. In some cases, the deception can be described as ludicrous, as when a vacuum cleaner was represented as "the best in the world…it had an activated charcoal air filter system...and would prevent colds, cause sound sleep and reduce air pollution." The initial offering prices for the vacuums were close to or no less than $500, reduced ultimately to a "bargain" $280 to $310. My wife and I buy vacuum cleaners today, more than 50 years later, for less than $100, though they don't prevent colds.

The Klamath tribal account, in an impressive showing of honesty, puts part of the blame on the natives themselves. Some of the money went to sensational purposes, the tribe admitted. "These became the fodder of the stories told in the press about huge days-long parties, multiple purchases of cars, and Indian individuals walking around with thousands of dollars in paper gags. Many of the stories were true. The fact that they were the exception did nothing to keep them marking all of the Klamath people as wild squanderers of their own relative wealth."

Gerald Skelton, cultural resources director for the Klamaths, told author Roberta Ulrich that alcoholism skyrocketed after tribal members received all that money. Five aunts, just young girls when getting more than $40,00 each in the 1960s, died young during termination, one after another dying, "what I remember growing up was going to a lot of funerals," he said. Skelton didn't say whether drinking helped cause their deaths, but he did say that alcoholism was a big part of how his mother "gets by" after receiving $100,000 in termination money and an inheritance as just a teenager. Others blame alcoholism for much of the physical and social dysfunction.

And why did some Klamaths suffer so much from their termination wealth? In its termination statement, the tribe contends that in being blamed for giving up their identity for the profits of their land sale, they developed feelings of guilt and frustration, causing them to get rid of the termination money that "symbolized their betrayal." The tribe did not say who or what led to the betrayal nor does it define what it means by "betrayal." Whatever the causes of the "betrayal," the Klamaths contend that it brought about "rampant alcoholism not to mention problems of suicide, domestic violence, loss of self-esteem and on and on." In other words, the Klamaths were dependent on sudden wealth, unprepared to deal with it, anxious to shed it and victims of it.

IV. Terminated

Tribal member Irwin Crume, as quoted in this author's account in 1959, had predicted that many of them would be victims, not only of the white merchants, but of themselves. "Very few manage their money the way they should. The majority will throw it away. That's the way they have lived all their lives. By golly, you can't even hire anybody anymore." Crume and his family needed to hire workers for raising cattle, sheep and horses on their 5,000-acre ranch. This author found, however, that some Klamaths "drove hard bargains and reaped good profits."

Overall, the FTC report saw the Klamaths as victims of outside forces, not of themselves. The agency came to this conclusion: "An urgent situation still exists in the Klamath community. Recent enforcement activities by the district attorney and Federal Trade Commission have not remedied the underlying social and economic problems of the Klamaths. Compensation for their loss of property does not eliminate the fact that they still have many of the problems faced by poor people. Unfair and fraudulent practices and lack of job opportunities and education can cause termination monies to rapidly disappear." Much of the money, the agency said, was spent on subsistence needs (not foolishly), some of it was ripped off, and whatever was restored was not necessarily enough to bring prosperity to tribal members.

Still, that analysis failed to mention that some Klamaths did invest their termination money wisely in education, business and for other purposes that produced long-term benefits.

Gordon Bettles and his family were among the wise ones. Bettles told this author that his father used termination money to buy a shopping center and set up a family business in real estate, while Gordon would go on to get degrees in two universities, including a master's degree in anthropology, international studies and linguistics. Clearly, Bettles knows the value of work, education, the wise use of money—and independence, a refusal to be dependent even on his tribe. In a family of 10, he saw his father work as a cowboy and logger, and along with his siblings took part in the work on their mother's ranch. "We had to do it to survive," he said. Bettles was encouraged to leave home, and he did. "All my life my parents said I had to

The Dependency Curse

be independent of what the tribe does; I have to take care of myself." It was good advice, because during the time of termination the tribe barely existed. Later, Bettles would work 17 years for the tribe, exploiting his education to create a culture center on what was left of the reservation. His children have followed his example. Most notably, two sons and a daughter are graduates of Cornell University in New York, working now in professional jobs.

Unlike Bettles, however, and more like the tribal member who bought the $28,000 car, many of the natives were spending their termination money—the equivalent of $1,000,000 per family in today's dollars—for short-term benefits. Oh no, the FTC said, "many of the withdrawing Klamaths have spent their termination money on basic necessities and have not been able to break out of their cycle of poverty because they could not find self-supporting income." As if that were the case, and it's a questionable assumption, the federal agency offered a somewhat bizarre recommendation: Provide welfare payments for the Klamaths so they could use their termination money, not for basic necessities, but to become self-supporting. (Perhaps that recommendation partly explains why the FTC issued this disclaimer on the cover of the regional office report: " This report has not been approved by the commissioners of the Federal Trade Commission and hence all statements, conclusions and recommendations contained herein do not necessarily reflect the official views of the commission."

In analyzing the report, one could ask, weren't the huge termination payments enough to meet basic needs as well as to make investments (like land and cattle) that would enable them to be self-supporting? The answer, said the FTC, is that when they received cash for their forest property they were misled to believe they were supporting themselves. (Figure that one out.) One could also ask, how could the Klamaths, receiving all that free money, qualify for welfare? The answer to that, said the FTC, would be to disregard the termination payments when calculating their welfare eligibility. In effect, pretend that they were still poor. Interesting. Think of the headline: "Many wealthy Indian families living on welfare."

As could be expected, this latest federal proposal, to put rich Klamaths on welfare, was not adopted, so it didn't give white critics something more

IV. Terminated

to carp about. Besides, the government did not totally abandon the once-dependent Klamaths or other terminated tribes. Under a relocation program, the government helped tribal members get housing, vocational training and employment in cities where jobs were available. Nor did the Klamaths abandon themselves, instead forming an "Organization of Forgotten Americans" to work for the benefit of a tribe that still existed even though it was forced to give up most of its reservation. That organization obtained federal and private money to help meet the legal, educational and health needs of the tribal members.

During termination, the Klamaths also were eligible for welfare and the other government benefits and services available to all citizens. Many who grew up in the cities, whether or not with the aid of the relocation program, made a success of their lives. Others, however, may have carried the curse of dependency from the reservation to the cities. They created urban Indian ghettos, became panhandlers and alcoholics and died too early. Sadly, we saw many of them in our city, Minneapolis. Hiroto Zakoji, who worked on educational programs for the Klamaths, conceded that a lot of those who moved to the cities had problems adjusting to the vast difference between life on the reservation and life in an urban setting. Some find it difficult to gain employment or apply for the local, state and federal benefits available for people of poverty or low incomes. After relying on familiar federal programs, they may not be familiar with the requirements for these local benefits. So some have turned to alcohol for a release from their failures.

Another effect of the move toward cities, reported the New York Times, "has been a proliferation of Native American street gangs, which mimic and sometimes form partnerships with better established African American and Latino gangs, according to the FBI." Later in this narrative, we'll look at one of those gangs in Minnesota, the notorious Native Mob, and one of its former members, Reuben Crowfeather.

But on their reservation, as well as in cities, the terminated Klamaths continued to endure the same social problems as they did while a self-sustaining tribe. Tom Ball, a descendent of the great Modoc freedom fighter Captain Jack, did health research on the tribe soon after it regained tribal

The Dependency Curse

status. In that research, part of his work on a doctor's degree, he found premature deaths, violent crimes and violent deaths as well as alcohol and substance abuse. In reservation town Chiloquin, Ball said he saw funeral after funeral, very few from old age or natural death. Of a dozen natives who died in Portland, he said, only two or three died of natural causes.[8]

Ball did more than describe the problems; he went on to be elected chairman in 1993 and attempt to deal with them, decrying tribal factionalism and calling for unity in providing for "future generations of the people," with "people" capitalized. (As we shall see later in this narrative, Ball was not the only leader to seek a unity of purpose in the Klamaths.) Yes, there were factions. As he wrote in the Klamath tribal newspaper, there were "withdrawing members, remaining members, the Crawford faction, the Jackson faction, traditional, Christian, educated, non-educated, from here, not-from here, Johnny come lately, outsider." Ball went to say, "These are all terms I have heard (and been called) by tribal members to describe ourselves. We even have two classifications of descendants, and even the 'splinter' group has a splinter group." (So much for the tendency of non-natives to lump the original Americans together as monolithic "Indians." They weren't all the same within a tribe, let alone among all the hundreds of tribes at many locations from east to west. Ball himself embodied the two classifications of descendants, Modoc and Klamath.)

For all the profound social problems, Ball also noted progress in the seven years since the Klamaths again became a federally recognized tribe: From a staff of four and a budget of almost nothing to a staff of 115 and a budget of more than $5 million, a nationally admired health program, improved housing, protection of burial grounds, a senior meals program and increased involvement in higher education, among other improvements.

Ball's understanding of the problems, meantime, was not to blame them on dependency—the Klamaths were not dependent on timber sales or the federal government during termination (but they were dependent on the big lump-sum payments) . Instead, in his doctoral dissertation he contended that 500 years of white colonialism and destructive federal policies— a form of dependency?—produced a "holocaust" leading to a debilitating

IV. Terminated

lifetime trauma for natives. (As we have noted, native scholar Yellow Horse Brave Heart earlier had come to the same conclusion.) As a result, Ball wrote, Indian people are at the bottom of every social indicator, from poverty, housing and education, to premature death, substance abuse, life expectancy and more. As one example, he noted that 58 percent of his research sample of Klamaths reported the death of a friend or family member from homicide. But he acknowledged that the small size of his sample, 98 natives or one-thirtieth of the Klamath population, limited the scope of his findings, suggesting, he concluded, that the trauma "may" have contributed to the negative social outcomes found in "some" American Indians. As the language he used makes clear, the findings were not conclusive.

Of course, nothing is conclusive about the causes or the cures of the continuing problems of the original Americans. Some Klamaths say termination made their condition worse, and fought to restore government support. After 26 years, they did.

Journalist Roberta Ulrich, in her research on Indian termination and restoration, generously shared with this author her interviews with Klamath people in early 2000, describing their horrible social problems, as well as their positive efforts to regain tribal stability. Yes, horrible social problems. We mentioned earlier how Jeff Mitchell's father went to prison and his children, including Jeff, went into the foster home of a Pentecostal minister and his wife in Chiloquin, center of the reservation. The foster parents also raised a number of Klamath children, sparing them the fate of many others who were sent out of the area. It should be remarked that other outside religious people also helped Klamath children prepare for successful lives. Mitchell went on to become tribal chairman.

(As a personal aside, my wife and I, along with other whites, were criticized in earlier years for "taking away" children from tribal families and adopting them, and the criticism had some validity because adoption agencies didn't do enough to recruit native families for adoption. But many of the children were not "taken away." Rather they needed new homes—adoptive or foster—as the neglected victims of dysfunctional native families, like the Mitchells.)

The Dependency Curse

Gail Chehak, a member of the committee that worked for government restoration, told Ulrich how the free money of termination similarly affected her family. Her divorced mother took up drinking after becoming independent with the termination money. She said that a lot of homes were destroyed that way. As a result, in that case, the mother lost her children, who went to foster care, to a grandmother and to a teacher, who later committed suicide. The Klamaths were terminated as a tribe, Chehak said, because the tribal members supposedly were able to manage their own affairs, but as soon as the money came, many were no longer able to do so. Gail was a victim of termination in another way: When she came of age to receive her $43,000 share of money, the bank, as trustee when she was a child, told her less than half was left. She took it and went on with her life, successfully.

The late Ramona Rank, an ordained Lutheran minister who also worked for restoration, told of some Klamaths who opposed restoration of tribal status, figuring they had adapted to mainstream life and didn't want anything more to do with the tribe. Some of the opposition was so intense, Rank said, that she received death threats.

Economist Trulove, who studied the Klamaths extensively, contended that, "In the long run, the termination was a good idea. To survive, Klamath had to enter the mainstream economy and develop useful workforce skills and acceptable social behavior. The reservation per capita (payments for timber sales) just allowed a dysfunctional lifestyle to continue. While the termination process was fundamentally flawed as the court rulings showed, people were forced to change their behavior more towards the more generally acceptable. For many Klamath the change was impossible but for some it provided a viable future." Overall, however, he concluded that termination provided few lasting benefits because tribal members chose to use the money to enhance their standard of living rather than to improve their workforce skills to obtain outside jobs.

Trulove could have added that termination also caused the Klamaths as a tribe to act on their own to sustain or improve their situation, without benefit of government aid. Relying partly on private money, the tribe, for

IV. Terminated

example, maintained a tribal constitution, tribal government (still active 20 years later) and a gaming commission. They also continued their legal actions to gain millions of dollars in additional compensation for the taking of their land. Further, they sought more money over the alleged failure of the government in earlier years to cut enough of their timber for per-capita payments.

At the same time, they went to court to affirm hunting, fishing and water rights, though no one claimed fish and game would make them self-sufficient.[9] In fact, by the 1940s said the government, "wildlife...is not so important when associated with the economy of the Indians. Only a few give very much time to the activities of hunting, trapping and fishing."[10]

One conclusion can be drawn from all this: Termination was not all bad, and, certainly, it was not all good.

So the question remains, what would it take for the Klamaths to be self-sufficient? As we've reported, many of the original Americans have answered that question by going from reservations to the cities, moving to compensate for lack of jobs and opportunities in their homelands, looking for a better life elsewhere. Nationally, the number of urban Indians has gone from 8 percent of the total native population in 1940 to 64 percent in 2000, as measured by the U.S. Census. In a three-decade period, from 1950 to 1980, an estimated 750,000 natives went to the cities. More than half the 3,670 Klamath tribal members have left their shrunken reservation and its environs. Even then, the reservation population is still greater than in the early 1900s.

For the Klamaths who remain on their reservation, self-sufficiency is an elusive goal. Tribal leaders contend that they can support themselves only if they get back their land. What they want, they say, is to heal the land and its resources, "and seek to restore them to some semblance of the abundance they once reflected," and to restore the spiritual integrity of their land. That would mean, presumably, training the natives as foresters, capable of managing their territory. A tall order, rewriting history; not easy to do. (The Klamaths make much of the spiritual and sacred connection between the people and the land, a gift from their creator. It must be said, however, that this bonding did not keep many Klamaths from selling their "sacred" land to non-Indians before termination.)

So far they are no closer to reaching the goal of self-sufficiency than when they regained their reservation status almost three decades ago. The problem is that they were paid handsomely for their land, and the government has shown no inclination to give it back. In 1992 the tribe promised to be self-sufficient if they got back their land, a proposal turned down by the government. In 2001 a newspaper headline said the Klamaths were negotiating to trade water rights to reclaim their lost land, but those negotiations broke down.[11] Lynn Schonchin, former tribal chairman (three times) and general manager, told this author that he doubted a land return was possible.

Give the Klamaths credit for trying. With timber no longer belonging to them, they have used their water resources as a bargaining chip to regain land and escape welfare dependency. Their water, tied to hunting and fishing treaty rights, is one of their last major assets. As noted elsewhere in this narrative, however, the Klamaths do not have unrestricted use of water in their region. Farmers, ranchers and salmon fishers also are competing for the water, primarily from three rivers and a lake in and south of the former reservation. Local farming and government interests have approved a complex water-sharing plan, including the removal of dams to enhance salmon runs, but Congress has balked at its cost. As part of it, conservationists have opposed return of most reservation land now in national forests, while, as noted, the Klamaths rejected a proposed land swap. On and on. So the tribe remains dependent on government.

CHAPTER V

Casino Dependency

YOU COULD CALL IT the millionaire's club with an unusual membership, of Native Americans, and with an improbable name, the Shakopee Mdewakanton Sioux Tribe of southern Minnesota. Each year each adult tribal member receives that much money for not working, and almost no one does work. Not bad for a once impoverished tribe of less than 500 members. The tribal president boasted a while back, smilingly, that because of casino wealth almost all of the members were unemployed, by choice.

What a contrast to the lives of the Sioux in the early 1800s, when they were part of the large Dakota nation whose tribes dominated much of Minnesota and the northern region, living off the fruit of the land, lakes and rivers. In a land of contending tribes, however, that bucolic life could not last, and didn't. First the Dakota would lose part of their homeland in battles with the rival Ojibway tribe. In fact, the Ojibways, or Chippewas as they were known then, had pushed them south and west, prompting the Dakotas, with muskets and steel knives acquired from white traders, to defeat or shoulder aside a succession of Plains tribes and build an empire of their own. But defeat is too soft a word. When necessary, according to one account, the Dakota resorted to "ruthless massacres" to build that empire. Leading them was the legendary Chief Red Cloud, known for his fighting qualities—reckless bravery, stealth, strength and imperviousness to personal danger.[1]

The Dependency Curse

Fast forward now to many years later when the empire, like many before it and since, was crumbling, this one under the rapid encroachment of white settlers, supported by the U.S. Army. Finally, in the death throes of the empire Red Cloud had built, a Dakota chief known as Little Crow negotiated a treaty with the government to give up 24 million acres of land. This was similar to what the Klamaths gave up under treaties to provide territories for the settlers. The alternative for the Dakota, wrote journalist Curt Brown in a comprehensive series of articles, appeared to be extinction for the once dominant nation of natives. It was a high price to pay, but their survival was at stake.[2]

According to Brown, "Little Crow was optimistic that in exchange for those huge tracts of land, the Dakota would acquire a strip of reservation land along the Minnesota River where at least they could still live as a sovereign nation. The $3 million the U.S. government put on the table would pay for food, schools, farming equipment, blacksmith shops and goods to ease his people into the new reality that seemed inevitable." Thus the Dakota, under Chief Little Crow, were willing to trade most of their land for a promised dependence on the government. And dependence it was. The Klamaths, after giving up most of their land, still had an immensely valuable forest to produce income upon which they could rely. The Dakota did not.

In no time at all, the Dakota were paying a terrible price for their dependence. They were barely able, or not able, to support themselves on the strip of reservation land, and the U.S government, embroiled in a costly civil war with the South, was episodic in fulfilling its promises to provide money and goods. Moreover, when the natives turned to white traders to buy necessary provisions, they were charged exorbitant prices, not just for necessities but also for alcohol that became a terrible addiction for them (and for so many other natives, as well as non-Indians, of course.). Oh, the tragic story continues. When the government did come through with committed money, the traders claimed much of it to repay debts. To add to the insult, the traders were fathering children with Dakota women, an affront to the native men.

V. Casino Dependency

By the summer of 1862, the Dakota were starving and seething after a bitter-cold winter when the government was late again in providing the promised provisions and "annuity payments." As a sign of their desperation, some of them broke into a government warehouse to get flour and other supplies. They also were embittered over the infamous statement of one of the traders, "If they are hungry, let them eat grass or their own dung."

With all that, it looked as if the Dakota were ready to go to war. But Little Crow was reluctant to do so. He hated the rapacious traders and the soldiers, but he did not hate all white people. He had been going occasionally to Episcopal services, performed by white missionaries seeking to convert the Dakotas to the white ways. And he knew about the Dakota faction that opposed war, having accommodated to the whites and adopted their farming methods. And he must have known that his people would lose such a war, lose so much. Most of all they would lose government support, a dependency that was restored and continues today.

Many of his people, especially the young warriors, however, wanted war, and they got it. So as the Modocs in Oregon would do later, they went to war in the late summer of that year against the soldiers and the settlers. "Propelled by years of broken promises, insults and watching their children starve to death on the reservation," wrote Brown. "Dakota fighters had gone to war with historic vengeance." And Little Crow was pleased that most of the first white victims were the corrupt traders he blamed for causing the war. "He also believed there was honor in his soldiers fighting U.S. soldiers, such as the two dozen ambushed and killed at the ferry crossing the first morning of war."

Like so many wars before and to follow, however, this one produced more victims than heroes. While sympathetic to the plight of the natives, Brown told the story straight on one of the largest massacres in the long history of the "Indian wars." As he described it, "Reluctantly leading the Dakota into battle was Little Crow. On Monday, Aug. 18, 1862, his fighters swept down on the settlers with speed and surprise, killing nearly everyone in their path—women, children and old people, as well as the swindling traders and soldiers Little Crow despised." The mutilated bodies of more

The Dependency Curse

than 200 settlers bloodied the prairie. Of course, Brown wrote, there was brutality on both sides, but he found nothing to compare with the mass killing by the Minnesota River.

In the end, as you would expect, the Dakota lost the war, most lost their reservation, and most lost their treaty rights to government assistance. There were minor skirmishes after that, but It was the last major conflict in those wars until, almost 30 years later, soldiers reacted to a minor provocation by opening fire on Lakota Sioux people at Wounded Knee Creek in South Dakota. They killed 150 civilians in a massacre rivaling the one perpetrated by the Sioux in Minnesota. The Minnesota Sioux suffered the worst reprisal of any native tribe, the mass execution by the government of 38 natives who had taken part in the killing of settlers. The next year Congress called for the removal of all Sioux from Minnesota, forcing them to scatter to nearby states and Canada. No soldiers went to the gallows for their part in the Wounded Knee massacre; in fact, 20 of them were awarded the Medal of Honor. The victims were just collateral damage in the government's relentless campaign to subdue the original Americans.

The Sioux were beaten but not exterminated, as one of the generals (Pope) had proposed. "The horrible massacres of women and children and the outrageous abuse of female prisoners, still alive, call for punishment beyond human power to inflict," Pope declared. "…It is my purpose utterly to exterminate the Sioux. They are to be treated as maniacs or wild beasts, and by no means as people with whom treaties or compromises can be made." (Only two of the Sioux were convicted of "violating females," Brown wrote.)

In his diatribe the general failed to mention that a large number of Sioux were opposed to the war, had adopted white farming methods, converted to Christianity and helped to protect the white settlers. They were sort of a peace party, as were some of the Modocs in Oregon in that war against the government. The extremist general also didn't consider the injustices that led the Sioux to go to war and massacre so many innocent settlers. (Fire-bombing in Japan and Germany, by the American military and its allies, took a far worse toll of civilians in World War II.)

V. Casino Dependency

Another military leader, Commandant Jacob Nix of New Ulm, was not so blinded by hatred as was Pope. Nix wrote in his history of the uprising, "One should not believe that the present generation of Indians has forgotten, or does not know, that the entire spacious territory of the U.S. once belonged to their ancestors and that their hunting grounds were alive and filled with all kinds of game. The savage knows this as well as we know it, and this the reason for his unforgivable hatred of the paleface, a hatred which only waits for the opportunity destroy the latter." Nix supported the execution of the native "criminals" but opposed making all the Indians pay for the wrongs committed by "specific individuals."

But most of them did pay, being banished from Minnesota and widely dispersed. What happened next, for more than 100 years, is an amazing story of resilience and survival. That part of the story, the focus of this narrative, involves a couple hundred Sioux who were not banished, who were allowed to remain in the state because they had cooperated with the army. For all their cooperation, however, the remaining Sioux got little more than a reprieve from banishment. According to their account, they subsequently "spent many impoverished years attempting to gain support and help from the government." Finally, in the 1890s Congress authorized the tribe to get back some of its land. Still, for more than 50 years thereafter life for the tribe was "one of poverty and hardship." Not until 1969 did the government recognize the Shakopee Sioux as an Indian tribe, making them qualified to receive all the benefits of that status. They wanted to be fully dependent again, and they were.

But less dependent in 1982, 120 years after the big war, when Sioux leader Norman Crooks established a bingo parlor, patterned after what he saw as the success of a bingo operation of the Seminole tribe in Florida. Ten years later the Shakopee tribe opened the casino—called Mystic Lake— that has grown to the point that all of the Sioux people are members of the millionaire's club, appropriately presided over by the late Stanley Crooks, Norman's son. And located, appropriately, near Shakopee, named after an Indian chief. By then their membership, after all the hardship, was a tiny fraction of what it was before their war. The years of poverty and "indepen-

The Dependency Curse

dence" had taken their toll.

The population of the tribe has since more than doubled, but not all by chance. A previous tribal president, Leonard Prescott, cousin of Stanley Crooks, wanted to restrict membership after he established the casino in 1992 (and restrict the sharing of profits?) Stanley Crooks beat him in the election that year, however, and opened up the tribal rolls to Sioux natives, regardless of whether they could prove a blood relationship. Prescott accused Crooks of stacking the electorate to win favorable votes, thus threatening to dilute the tribe beyond distinction. It was a classic political fight, mirrored in Republican efforts now to restrict voters to favor their party. And it was a fight that continued for many years, as we will note later.

The bigger issue now, as raised before in this account, is whether the astounding wealth of the Shakopee Sioux, and some of the other gambling tribes, is the answer to the endemic social problems of Native Americans? Is this dependence on unearned casino money better than dependence on unearned government money? Not entirely. As we have learned in the research for this narrative, overwhelming wealth can cause crippling complications, involvements and expectations, not to mention the loss of the needed initiative to achieve a good life.

Talk about complications. Millionaire Daniel Edwin Jones owns two homes, a Mercedes-Benz with driver, a second car and a fishing boat, making him one of America's 1 percent without ever working for it. But a recent news story reported that he was swimming in debt, one home in foreclosure and supposedly unable to make payments on $2 million owed, in a court settlement, to the family of a 16-year-old girl who died of a drug overdose after he prevented others from calling for help. Jones spent four years in prison on a conviction of criminal sexual assault and related crimes for having sex with the victim, Brittany Powell, when she was helpless from the drug overdose. He was 18 at the time; had his own problems with drugs and alcohol. More recently, according to one account, "Jones has been flashing his deep pockets and disrespect for Brittany's family by showing up to court in a black limousine and making snide remarks as he leaves the courtroom."[3] Did anyone say he was a nice guy?

V. Casino Dependency

Or consider the involvements of Reuben Crowfeather, a crime-prone native who acquired access to the Sioux millions by living with a member of the tribe. At the same time, he was a member of the notorious Native Mob gang, described by the government as one of the most dangerous gangs in the country. Crowfeather would be busted for drug dealing and possessing six firearms, a possession his gang sought for use in criminal activity. He went to prison for more than five years for that crime, after partying with a gang boss at the casino.[4] Crowfeather's actual involvement in the gang activities has not been demonstrated, but after leaving prison he went on the internet to invite natives to be "part of the solution," not the problem, vowing to stay sober and even die or kill for his "people." He gave a phone number but did not return calls from this author. A local police official said he appeared to be posing as a reformer. Maybe, or maybe he was sincere, responding to a lecture from the judge in his case.

And don't overlook the expectations of Mary Welch, also an outsider, who sought permanent—yes, permanent—financial support from her millionaire Sioux husband upon their separation after more than a decade living on casino wealth, without working. A tribal court ruled that she had a right to receive part of her husband's casino money to support their son until he became 18, but no right to forever maintain a "very high standard of living," that included monthly payments of $1,000 for entertainment and recreation, $850 for the boarding care of her two horses, $500 for a housekeeper and $300 for eating out. Her husband's annual income of almost $1 million from the tribe certainly should have been enough to cover such expenses, but no, the court noted that extensive debts demonstrated an "inflated standard of living, to some extent."[5]

Bottom line: The $1 million had not been enough to support the Welches, any more than it was enough for Jones to make payments on his court settlement. Jones told the court he was "cash-strapped," dependent on his wife's family for basic necessities.

This author does wonder, however, whether the beautiful young women who hook up with aged tycoons on the expectation that, sometimes under contracts, they will get settlements upon divorce or death that will assure them of a luxury lifestyle the rest of their lives. The tribal court figured that Welch's husband, Alan, could count on receiving $50 million from the tribe in his remaining years, even then a pittance compared to the financial futures of the billionaires.

It would be unfair, of course, to mention that American Indians expect to continue receiving, forever, billions of dollars from the federal government each year, for the taking of their land more than a century ago. They have treaty rights to receive that compensation. It could be mentioned, unfairly perhaps, that the descendants of African slaves, whose freedoms were taken away, don't get any reparations from the government, and this father's two fiercely independent adopted sons—of African and native lineage—don't want any such money.

Or is it unfair to say such things? At least one reader of the story about Jones doesn't think so, writing that "I see no reason they should have a monopoly on something (the casino) just because of what was done to their ancestors who most of them probably can't even trace back. If that is the case, why aren't the (descendants) of slaves being given $900,000 a year, too?...He ((Jones) makes more in one month than I do in a year and he can't pay his bills? Maybe they should garnish it from the tribe. Oh wait—they have their own tribal laws and council so they can't. Stupid!"[6]

Of course, one cannot rely on the anecdotes of Jones, Crowfeather and Welch in one tribe to reach any conclusions about the merits (or demerits) of casino gambling for native people. It's better to look at the big picture, at the impact of the casinos on the 100,000 natives in Minnesota, as portrayed by teacher Steve Date (a Native American) and journalist Sharon Schmickle on the news website Minnpost. They ask the question, has the money from 18 casinos in one state, 20 years in the making, improved lives on Minnesota's Indian reservations? Their answer: For a few, emphatically yes; for others, somewhat so; for most, not at all. Casino money has enabled some of the Indian tribes to make enough money to improve housing, education and social programs, but not enough to bring them into the middle-class mainstream of life. And some of the tribes have no casinos or what they have are too small or too remote to make much of a difference. Compared with the

V. Casino Dependency

over-all Minnesota population, native incomes, despite dramatic gains, are still lower, while educational attainment, poverty and jobless rates remain higher. In fact, up north where most Minnesota Indians have their roots, casino profits have been too slim even to lift families out of poverty, write Date and Schmickle. If they make enough money, some tribes provide modest per-capita payments to their members; some do not. In summary, the casino experience in Minnesota shows that casino gambling is no panacea over-all for native Americans. And that is a no-brainer.[7]

Judge James Randall of Minnesota, a leading critic on native affairs, summed it up this way in a legal brief: "If we are honest, we must concede that hopes for a thriving multi-million-dollar casino like Mystic Lake or Foxwood (in Connecticut) on every reservation, to cure all ills, is no hope at all. There is no guarantee the few eminently successful Indian casinos will have the ability forever to continue at their present levels." He wrote this two decades ago, and "forever" has already arrived, as will be reported in this account.[8]

Even at the extreme, there is no doubt that casino wealth has been a mixed blessing even for the Shakopee Sioux tribe in Minnesota. On the one hand, the late tribal president Crooks told the Star Tribune of Minneapolis that younger tribal members were becoming undisciplined and spoiled because gambling robbed their need or desire to work.[9] According to the report in the New York Times, families say it is difficult to teach children the value of money when everyone knows no one will likely ever need to work. Beyond the effect on children or young people, a Shakopee gaming supervisor reported seeing bad checks, gambling addiction and lots of alcohol and drug problems.[10]

On the other hand, casino profits enabled vast improvements in the economic status and living conditions for Shakopee Sioux tribal members, as well as making it possible for some members to go into business. Decades earlier, they lived in beat-up trailer homes, lacked indoor plumbing and survived on food stamps. Now, according to the Times report, many have expensive cars, own second homes away from their reservation, send their children to private schools, enjoy expensive hobbies such as thoroughbred

The Dependency Curse

breeding, go big-game hunting and take elaborate trips.[11]

Beyond that, says the tribe, it provides a full range of services for the general welfare of its members, as required by federal law. This includes health and dental care, social-service and educational programs. The tribe also provides water and sewage treatment, fire protection and road maintenance. And then there are the enterprises: a championship golf course, three hotel towers, restaurants, RV park, wind-turbine and energy plant. In all, the tribe provides thousands of jobs for members and non-tribal people to support these services and businesses.[12]

Native author David Treuer observes, wryly, that while "income" for the Sioux people is growing, so is the size of their houses, 38 percent supersize with nine bedrooms or more. The only figures not growing rapidly, he writes in "Rez Life," are high school graduation rates (below 50 percent) and Indians with college degrees (5 percent).[13]

Meantime, the authoritative Study Commission on Native American Gaming challenges the many claims of jobs created among casino tribes: "The issue of economic benefit is…complicated by the fact that much of this accrues not to the tribes or their members but to outside individuals, such as non-Indian locals who usually comprise the overwhelming majority of workers in Indian casinos, and the non-Indian corporations which are the usual operators of the casinos."[14]

Aside from per capita payments, many other natives and causes have enjoyed the benefits of the casino gambling. The Minnesota tribe has donated and loaned more than $700 million to other tribes, charities and even a university football stadium, all in the 20 years of its Mystic Lake casino business.

As you might expect, the Shakopee Sioux spend generously of their profits to protect a casino monopoly guaranteed by the state. They are the biggest players in a lobbying consortium of Minnesota's Indian gaming tribes that has given more than $6 million in political donations in recent years, as reported by Tony Kennedy in the Star Tribune of Minneapolis. (The Shakopee tribe has spent $3 million on lobbying since 1998.) Under their compact with Minnesota, the 18 Indian casinos share none of the $600

V. Casino Dependency

million they earn annually. The newspaper called it an "epic gambling fight."

In another move to avoid competition, the Shakopee tribe agreed to pay $75 million over 10 years to the nearby Canterbury Downs horse-racing track. You can bet that the ailing Canterbury track won't be seeking to add slot machines in so-called racino gambling to compete with Mystic Lake.[15]

The Minnesota tribes fought back in the "epic gambling fight," noting in a rebuttal article in the Star Tribune that much of its gambling revenue goes to prize payouts. Working with lobbyists is the responsible thing to do, the tribes wrote. "Without gaming, we would not come close to meeting our people's needs. Even with gaming, tribal governments still struggle to meet important needs and some tribal members will go without the basics that most Minnesotans take for granted." The tribes in their statement did not mention the gambling money that makes millionaires of the Shakopee Mdewakanton Sioux tribal members.

But the reader should not be surprised to learn that the Shakopee Sioux have been lobbying to protect what they have, a rather typical purpose of all lobbying, of corporations, labor unions and do-good organizations.

While some tribes like the Shakopee Sioux still reap handsome profits, the odds are not so good that other tribes—or even the Sioux— can maintain their generous payments to members or count on gaming as a sole source of revenue. The Sioux, for example, had to cut back 30 per cent on donations to other tribes because the recent economic recession reduced their casino earnings.[16] Indian casinos also face increasing competition from commercial gaming and even rival native casinos. The New York Times, in its article on the Shakopee Sioux, carried a headline, "1 Million Each Year for All, Until Tribe's Luck Runs Out."

Across the country, The Klamaths got into trouble on plans to enlarge their small casino, losing $2 million in front money when they had to cancel an expansion because of the recession and lack of financing. The Klamaths, like other isolated tribes, make very little in profits from their casino, contrary to the tribes in urban areas with big gambling markets.[17] Still, a desire for more casino payments helped bring about a rebellion against tribal

The Dependency Curse

leaders. More on this later in this narrative.

(The Klamaths were lucky to lose so little. In Connecticut, the casino dependency collapsed for the 450 natives who were each receiving $100,000 or more a year from their immensely profitable Foxwoods casino, largest Indian casino in America. But when the Mashantucket Pequot tribe went $2 billion into debt from excessive borrowing to expand the casino, it cut off the payments to tribal members and created a food pantry to provide meals for needy natives.)[18]

Like many other tribes, the Klamaths don't make enough from their small casino to provide any significant payments to members and thereby create that kind of a dependency. As we've noted, however, after the government terminated them as a tribe, they fought for and succeeded in restoring tribal status to regain their previous dependence on federal funds. They also want to get back their land, a dubious prospect considering, as pointed out earlier, they were paid $220 million for their forested reservation, along with additional millions from separate legal actions for land lost.

The Klamaths became one-time millionaires, in today's dollars, from the sale of their land 50 years ago; the Shakopee Sioux receive that much every year from the gamblers, most not so rich, who also seek unearned money, if not a quick fortune.

The wealth of the few gambling-rich tribes like the Shakopee Sioux mirrors the wealth of the American 1 percent, a potent political issue of economic inequality, a long-time but growing problem in the country. The disparity between super-rich Indians and most other natives is of recent vintage. "At the end of the 1980s, in a frenzy of cost cutting and privatization," explain investigative reporters Donald Barlett and James Steele, "Washington perceived gaming on reservations as a cheap way to wean tribes from government handouts, encourage economic development and promote tribal self-sufficiency."[19]

For the Sioux, however, dependence on gaming could be viewed as a curse as well as a well-demonstrated cure. It has indeed produced tribal self-sufficiency. But as we have noted in this narrative it also has eliminated the incentive for the natives to get an education and a job, causing some to turn

V. Casino Dependency

to drinking and drugs to compensate for empty lives. It has led to feuds and fights for control over the lucrative gambling business, as seen in conflict between cousins Prescott and Crooks. It has complicated the lives of tribal members and their partners (like Jones, Crowfeather and Welch). It has burdened the tribal court with endless litigation (in one case, plaintiffs seeking tribal membership filed a complaint, amended complaint, supplemental complaint and second supplemental complaint).

As could be expected, moreover, unfettered spending by the Shakopee tribe has caused conflict in the nearby city of Prior Lake. Some officials of the city have opposed tribal purchase of large tracts of land and putting it into federal trust status, thus taking it off the tax rolls and jeopardizing economic development.[20] Tribal officials respond that they need the land for their own economic development for the benefit of their members. And some white residents, reflecting perhaps an inbred racism, speak disgustingly of the "'fat cats" on the reservation. Indian people are not supposed to be wealthy. Most in the nation are not. (Maybe mindful of the potential for a white "backlash," Crooks sought to build bridges with broader white communities.)

Around the country, the incentive for many tribes is to maintain or increase their dependence on casino gambling, rather than worry about the negative side effects, as shown in the Shakopee Sioux. Like the Sioux they put much of the money into programs to improve their economic and social condition. On the other hand, some tribes, often the prosperous ones, seek to avoid competition from other tribes, often the less prosperous ones. A few are seeking to establish casinos off their reservations and nearer to population centers, which requires government approval. Or they dis-enroll members to avoid sharing casino profits. Or they play the race card to oppose non-Indian commercial gambling. Or spend millions on lobbying, political contributions or lawsuits to retain their privileged status. According to one report, casino payments allegedly are even an incentive for some white women to get pregnant by Indian men and produce "dividend babies" for a share of the gambling profits. Over-all, these profits amounted to an astounding $5 billion in a recent year, most of it going to the few tribes with super-casinos near population centers.[21]

A big issue for the gambling tribes, and an underlying cause of the infighting, is how much, or whether, to pay individual members from those casino profits. Those per capita payouts were tellingly described a while back by Leland McGee, a member the Oklahoma Cherokee nation, as a big mistake, "nothing short of a tribally funded 'welfare state.'" McGee, who is worth quoting in full: "Per capita has become something so adverse amongst so many of our people that it now serves to hinder, disrupt and in some instances, even dismantle tribal governments. Disenrollment, political turmoil, government breakdowns, corruption, financial dependency and absolute greed has become the new 'norm' for too many gaming tribes." He adds, "We have families pitted against families fighting over who is and who is not a rightful citizen of their tribal government." And in many cases, he says, tribal citizens threaten to oust leaders who don't satisfy their thirst for more and more "free money."[22]

As an example, David Wilkins, a native scholar at the University of Minnesota, has counted native nations in 17 states engaging in an expanding disenrollment practice. The Nooksack tribe in Washington state, he wrote, was moving to dispel roughly 15 percent of that nation's 2,000 members. Applied to the United States, that would mean a reduction of about 45 million people.[23]

Coming home from the West Coast, my wife and I drove through the territory of the Oklahoma Cherokee, one of 566 native tribes scattered across the country, representing so many cultures, populations and economic classes, from one of the poorest at Pine Ridge to the relatively well-off Cherokee. I am particularly interested in the Cherokee because they are in the middle of the classic dependency conflict over those per capita payments. The Oklahoma Cherokee provide no such payments, while the eastern band, the North Carolina Cherokee, do provide them to members.

Why not in Oklahoma? The Cherokee in that state answer the question this way: While a few native tribes (actually, somewhat less than one-fourth of them) have chosen to disburse gaming revenues directly to their citizens, "Cherokee Nation has chosen instead to invest our gaming revenue to help

V. Casino Dependency

educate, employ and assist Cherokee Nation citizens" through such programs as health, housing and community services. McGee has credibility to discuss the issue not only as a member of the second largest tribe in the country, but also because of his self-described background as a native gaming and economic consultant, service in Indian affairs under the Clinton and Bush administrations, director of government affairs for a national Indian law firm and service as an official of tribal governments. (The pros and cons of per capita payments to tribal members, especially from timber sales, also are discussed at length in Chapter 4.)

To the east, the North Carolina Cherokee have taken a different path, providing per capita payments to members from its large casino enterprise, but at a cost. The eastern Cherokee incurred a huge debt in spending $633 million to enlarge its casino operation a few years ago, and has broken ground on a new resort and gambling facility, at a cost of $62 million. The eastern Cherokee have been paying almost $8,000 a year to each tribal member, which is a modest amount but not so modest at $168,000 for children when they reach age 18; their annual payments held in trust until then. (I like the requirement that young members must graduate from high school to get the money; otherwise they must wait until age 21.) With only 12,500 members—a fraction of the population of the Oklahoma Cherokee—the eastern band can afford per capita payments as well as improvements in housing (replacing trailers, no less), schools and utilities, and providing two health clinics, community facilities and college scholarships. As we have noted, the Shakopee Sioux in Minnesota with fewer than 500 members, have tons of money for everything and everybody, showing the wide disparity in the spread of casino wealth.

In all fairness, it should be pointed out that some natives see the per capita payments, not as a negative dependency, but as a move to greater independence, a freeing up from government benefits and control. For the shareholders in the tribal estate, they say, the payments are the same as stock dividends and capital gains for many Americans (money that many have not earned). Those payments, they note, have taken many of them out of poverty and into prosperity.[24]

The Dependency Curse

The Native Nations Institute for Leadership, Management and Policy at the University of Arizona listed these common arguments, among others, for the per capita payments: They help native citizens, critically short of cash, meet urgent needs. They shift decisions on use of the cash from tribal governments, some of whom waste money, to these individual citizens. And they are an equalizer, a leveler of the playing field, in many tribal nations that favor a few on jobs, services and housing, leaving others to fend for themselves. Urgent needs? The institute noted that immediately after each payout, one tribal court was inundated by parents filing petitions to collect overdue child-support payments from ex-spouses, another court by parents petitioning for access to their children's per-capita payments held in trust accounts.[25]

Seeking such benefits, many natives put pressure on tribal leaders to expand the payments. The late Marge Anderson knew the hazards of rebuffing this thirst for what critics call "free money." She was twice ousted as leader of the Mille Lacs Band of Ojibwe in Minnesota for her opposition to the per capita payments for 3,500 members, figuring that the payments would have to be divided among so many people the money "would be gone overnight," according to an article in the Star Tribune. She used the profits from two casinos for social programs, schools and a health clinic. As she saw it, tribal government should help members learn a trade or profession, so they can return to help their people. Melanie Benjamin, who campaigned to share more money with members, defeated Anderson in the year 2000, and then, after an Anderson comeback, beat her again in 2008. Even then, Mill Lacs leaders provide a relatively small $900 a month in per capita payments, and, concerned about student motivation, prohibit young people from withdrawing their money on their 18th birthdays unless they've earned a high school diploma. Anderson's Mille Lacs band also is diversifying its economy, as proposed by McGee, by buying hotels in downstate St. Paul.[26]

What can or should be done—if anything—about the payments? It's critical, contends McGee, for tribes to do a better job of educating their people as to the pitfalls of "per capita dependency." There's that word again, dependency. And this author would contend that it's not just a dependency

V. Casino Dependency

on the per capita payments. It's also a dependency on an ever expanding casino business (read Cherokee here) to feed the needs of tribal governments and their electorate, as well as to make per capita payments. Remember that the Foxwoods casino in Connecticut defaulted on a $2 billion debt and had to cut off per capita payments. And it could get worse. The realist McGee warns that the Indian casino monopoly is fragile as states allow non-Indian gaming to boost tax revenues, thus causing a "devastating" impact on "a large percentage of Indian gaming as we know it." That threat hasn't stopped McGee's own tribal nation, the Oklahoma Cherokee, from spending $52 million to add a third hotel tower to its Tulsa casino. Nor has it kept the North Carolina Cherokee from planning to spend $62 million to add a second hotel at their gaming enterprise, although to get state approval it agreed with its governor to increase the state's share of their revenue.

The Shakopee Sioux in Minnesota aren't worrying about their future, yet. With a huge revenue stream and a tiny membership, they've had it both ways, million-dollar payments to members (perhaps a detriment?) and million-dollar outlays for social and economic development programs (a benefit). The Oklahoma Cherokee, one of the largest tribes in the country, haven't even tried to make millionaires out of their 100,000 members, even if they could with eight casinos. As with the Cherokee, the gambling uncertainty has not deterred the Red Lake Band of Ojibwe Indians in Minnesota and the Confederated Tribes of Warm Springs of Oregon from expanding their casino operations, even though both are located a considerable distance from any large population centers. For the isolated Red Lake band, this is the third small casino no less. Tribal leaders hope that a hotel and upscale restaurant at the gambling site will attract players from nearby small-town Bemidji and the surrounding area, thereby increasing revenue to repay debt, nurture other businesses and finance infrastructure improvements. Playing catch-up, Warm Springs is building a second casino at its reservation. The Warm Springs are considered one of the more successful tribes economically, from timber and electricity production, even though it remains beset by "staggering" social problems. But the economic recession took its toll there, too, prompting the tribe to phase out its small casino and build a fancy establishment in the expectation it will significantly increase revenues by up to four times as a resort destination.

As we have shown, however, casino gambling will not solve the tragic social pathologies of most Native Americans. The biggest reason is that less than 40 percent of the tribes have casinos, and a tiny percent make big money from their gambling. Nevertheless, Angela Gonzales, assistant professor at Cornell University and a member of the Hopi tribe in Arizona, emphasizes the advantages of gaming for the tribes that sponsor it. "There is little doubt that tribal gaming has been more successful than all previous anti-poverty programmes in creating jobs, reducing welfare dependency and holding the promise of a bright future for some Indian tribes and their members," she writes.[27] In addition to all that, these tribes have transformed their images from pre-gambling poverty to big-time generators of wealth, a wealth many share with local and state governments, other tribes and non-Indian causes, a sharing partly in self-interest of maintaining their gambling monopolies.

The late Minnesota Ojibwe writer Jim Northrup offered another version of the casino dependency almost a century ago, thusly: "According to Donald Trump, Indian casinos are ripe for a takeover by organized crime. In his testimony before Congress, Trump said the mob has already infiltrated casinos run by Indians. However, he could offer no proof other than everyone is talking about it. Here on the Fond du Lac Reservation, we don't have to worry about organized crime—it is the unorganized crime we have to worry about."

How prescient. How telling of the corruption soon to be exposed in a casino run by a tribal leader in Minnesota, without any help from the mob. And how self-serving for the now presidential candidate Donald Trump, who had to worry already then about Indian competition for his own casinos.

CHAPTER VI

Klamaths Today

FOR THE FIRST TIME, these contrasting life stories of the original Americans—of the Klamaths and Mdewakanton Shakopee Sioux—raise the question, are they the victims or the beneficiaries of dependence on government and now on gambling? In short, can this dependence be blamed, at least partly, for the social problems suffered by so many of the native people? That's the question some of them are asking.

The Klamaths have not been so fortunate as the millionaire gambling Sioux tribe in Minnesota. While some invested a one-time fortune wisely, many did not, and now, isolated, lacking in land, resources and a big-time casino, they depend largely on the government for support. In fact, within five years after each had received the equivalent of $1 million, almost 40 percent of them had nothing left of their fortune.[1] Of course, that is hardly unusual for those of any race who receive an unprecedented amount of money, especially when they are new to sudden riches.

But the story of the Klamath tribes, as told by Klamaths, not outsiders, is worth considering because it addresses the key questions for the native people of America: What are the causes of their widespread social pathology and what can be done about it? Those problems have continued for the Klamaths through three major phases, from their dependence on timber sales for family income, to termination of their reservation, casting them into the mainstream of society, to a return to tribal status and dependence on the federal government for major benefits.

And today, the government does not protect them from a harsh reality. As described by tribal member Mario Sampson: "People are running rampant," dealing drugs out of their homes, drinking alcohol to excess. Some dealers, "out of their mind" on drugs, smash into his Chevy; one then gets a job in the tribal health program. Certain families are maintaining a monopoly on jobs, not doing their work but not being fired. A tribal official acts as if he is God, works only when he feels like it. Many Klamaths don't care about tribal business, going to a meeting for a free lunch but too few staying for a quorum to do business. If that were not enough, he says, there is an underlying problem of prejudice and division within the tribe. Sampson said he was "not happy with what is going on with our tribe."[2]

Is Sampson a credible critic? When asked that question, former tribal chairman Tom Ball said, "Mario Sampson has lived in the community, raised his children in Chiloquin (the reservation town), so he has a unique community perspective, although that view point is sometimes very narrow and lacks a deeper understanding of why these problems exist, and how they came to be." Tribal elder Lynn Schonchin added, "I like Mario Sampson. He's up front, tells you what he thinks. Tells it like it is."

Sampson was not the only insider, either, to criticize fellow Klamaths. Tribal member Catherine Weiser observed, "You can watch the people who get the GA's (welfare, general assistance), cash their checks and buy beer all day."

And Steve Lang had said earlier that "he felt, and a lot of people feel, that restoring the sucker (fish) program is like throwing money down a bathtub…younger people don't even know what a sucker is." He proposed that the tribe put more money into housing; others expressed the need for more jobs, not the saving of a fish species like the sucker, as tribal leaders were proposing. He said he felt the staff and management were supporting the project out of self-interest.[3] In fact, despite a defense of the sucker program (see below), the tribe has conceded that suckers were endangered and for a long time had prohibited tribal members from taking two species

VI. Klamaths Today

of the fish.[4] Restoration of the sucker resource is a top priority for the tribe. A tribal council resolution would declare later, "The Klamath Tribes has a long intertwined history with...the suckers...The cascade springs historically supported thousands of spawning suckers and now are believed not to support any."[5]

Tribal chairman Charles Kimbol also defended the sucker program as part of Klamath history: "Suckers were one of the staples of the Klamath diet for 14,000 years...Two of three species are currently endangered and if we lose them we'll lose them forever...It is our responsibility as tribal people to preserve these fish. If we don't, we are giving up a right that we fought in the courts for many years to maintain and retain. If our young people don't know what suckers are...it is because we have gradually been losing them to the point of extinction."[6] In a way, it was a defense of the past, even a dependency that no longer existed. Cheryl Tupper, manager of the tribe's natural resources office, said so, implicitly: "This is a treaty right we have to maintain." One could ask, why the sucker? As a food source, once again? Do the Klamath people want it or is it a symbol of their past? According to a survey of members and what they say, it may well be they prefer jobs, education and housing instead. After termination, more than half were unemployed.[7] "Jobs are important to all of us; we gain self-esteem and have a brighter future," said Sampson, lamenting a familiar complaint, that nepotism controls employment in tribal government.[8]

Without looking to the past, the Klamaths are mostly dependent in the present, on grants from the government, making them a "grant economy,' as another member put it. And is this dependence partly the cause of the social problems of the Klamaths, as described by Sampson? Joe Skahan, a Klamath of middle age, son of activist Barbara Alatorre, who lives off the reservation, thinks so. "You can't just live in separation and have everything handed to you," he says. This dependency, he added in an interview, causes people to be depressed and turn to drinking to overcome it. "Some do it (drink) to get away from the problems. I go back and forth to the reservation. There is more of a problem in the reservation than in society. Some who stay get down on themselves. So they drink. Like for everyone else there are pressures from family and friends. If they don't get bigger and better, they start feeling bad about themselves. They think (by drinking) they can forget. But they don't. Others remind them." (Skahan is not a psychologist, but he could be.)

If dependency is part of the problem, as other natives also contend, neither Sampson nor Skahan are among its victims. Sampson, at a meeting of the tribal council, pointed out that he worked in the private sector for 37 years, much of it as an ironworker. He appeared before the council not for himself, he said, but because he was "fighting for my kids and grandkids." Sampson even apologized for coming to drop "the bomb" of problems on the council. Newly elected tribal chairman Gary Frost was sympathetic: "Come anytime; I will listen. I hear a lot of concerns." Frost had been elected as a result of the revolt against past leaders. As for Skahan, he has two jobs in big-city Portland, far removed from the influences of reservation life.

Sampson's dark view of the tragedies of life among original Americans is not unusual, but neither is it, in many cases, representative of the 3,670 Klamath people—or of natives nationally. Other Klamaths, like Barbara Alatorre, Thomas Ball, Lynn Schonchin and Gordon Bettles, have built successful careers and worked to improve the lives of fellow natives. They are not victims of circumstances or of dependency; they are positive examples of forces of change at work in native communities across America. As such, they insist on maintaining native culture and identity in the tradition of other nationalities.

Typically, however, they go beyond the romantic view of many white people, that natives generally are close to nature and the land, caring of their families, continuing a harmonious past. Many natives, like Mario Sampson, are more realistic than idealistic about tribal life. Sampson didn't mention all the negatives. Others tell of children taken away from drugged-up mothers, too many natives dying young, committing suicide or going to prison because of alcohol and drugs, too many dying in traffic accidents. You'll find the true feelings of the Klamaths and other natives across the country in their newsletters, websites, meeting reports and in interviews.

And you'll learn of their contentious politics, as part of the American

VI. Klamaths Today

tradition, in the violence that erupted at Klamath meetings over efforts by three women to recall tribal leaders, including chairman Joe Kirk, because of perceived problems in the tribe. It got so bad that sheriff's deputies and state troopers were called in three times to restore order, once when up to 15 people were "fighting or trying to break up fighting while dozens more watched," according to the local newspaper. The women complained about the low payments from casino revenue, along with what they considered to be minimal services, poor communication with members, and a common complaint: nepotism. GeorGene Nelson, a construction secretary and legal advocate for the tribe, spoke for the rebels when she declared, "There are high levels of frustration amongst people who do not work for the tribes," but are the people who wrote the tribal laws that govern the land and resources and protect their inherent rights.

Chairman Kirk, member of the elder Seldon Kirk family, responded: "…it appears that the legal process is not sufficient for some members of this group, and they have resorted to the use of intimidation and unlawful action to try to have their way—they have even come to the administration offices and set up what people would call a stakeout over the past two days." The rebels lost their effort to recall the leaders, but succeeded in the next election in ousting them. It was self-determination with a vengeance, as defined by those in the government and outside of it, all within a mode of dependence.

The big question is whether the new Klamath leaders on their own will be able to make much of a difference in solving the problems the women raised or the more profound problems cited later by Mario Sampson and other critics. Most of the bigger problems have persisted through much of the past century, regardless of changes in leadership or tribal situation, of dependency or no dependency, not just for the Klamaths in the environs of their small reservation, but also for many of the Klamaths—more than half of its members—who live in cities, small towns and rural areas elsewhere.

If dependency was part of the of the problem for the Klamaths earlier, it wasn't a factor during almost three decades of termination when many tribal members were left to rely on themselves or on the social benefits available to all citizens in need. That's when, in the early 1960s as we have noted, the U.S. government, in an experiment to assimilate natives into the mainstream culture, stripped away the tribal status of the Klamaths, bought their timber and provided the huge onetime payments. Nationally, the experiment involved less than one-fifth of the tribes, with 13,000 members—3 percent of the native population; all have since been restored to tribal status. (For a long time, the American government has sought either to assimilate natives or separate them on reservations.)

Why did the Klamath's problems continue after termination? Scholar Ball's findings, conclusive or not, led him to contend that the Klamaths suffered a "double whammy" of "termination trauma" as well as a lifetime trauma for all natives over the loss of their lands. And his findings are just as relevant today, almost three decades after the Klamaths regained tribal status—in 1986. By many measures they are an ailing society: Welfare payments have increased at twice the rate of increase in inflation. Unemployment went up more than twice the rate in the non-Indian population. The percentage of child victims of abuse is reported to be four times the rate for white children in Klamath county, where their reservation is located. The percentage of native children taken from their parents and placed in foster care is almost six times the white rate.

And then there are the early deaths. The alcohol-related death of Ian Hoches-Bettles at age 34, prompted his step-mother Lynn Bettles to note that drinking has a role in the deaths of "so many of our young people." In his honor, she started an awareness project to help spare the lives of other natives. Tribal member Rose Mary Treetop, at a council meeting, also referred to Klamaths addicted to drugs and alcohol, saying, "I pray for them to change their lifestyle; they are crying out for help and we need to help them."[9]

As could be expected, dependency and Ball's theory of post-termination and lifetime trauma are hardly the only possible causes put forth to explain the plight of the natives, especially the abuse of alcohol and drugs that underlies so many of the social problems. Other researchers, and natives themselves, cite a possible genetic predisposition to drinking, along with poor self-image, lack of cultural and parental controls, peer or social pres-

VI. Klamaths Today

sure, poverty, high unemployment and low school-completion rates. A significant body of evidence, including a large study in Denmark, points to genetics as a major factor in alcoholism, suggesting an interplay between heredity and environmental factors.[10] The environmental factors include high unemployment and low school-completion rates, according to one expert. The result: Indian drinkers bond with each other, a reflection of the power of the peer group. A review of the research and expert opinion, however, shows there is no consensus on the causes of the debilitating alcoholism in native tribes. In fact, an "addiction blog" on the internet asked the question, "Is Native American alcoholism genetic?" And answered it, "We don't know."

Whatever the causes, alcohol induced death of natives is six times the national average. Homicides are double; suicide almost double.

But not all Native Americans have suffered from the alcohol affliction, raising questions about their alleged genetic propensity to drink excessively. The Pawnees, for example, "remained a remarkably temperate people, and their abstinence was widely remarked upon on the plains," says researcher White. And why did they reject liquor while other natives, including the Klamaths, did not? "Much of the answer lies in the ability of the chiefs to retain control of the trade" as determined by their culture, White explains.[11] So much for the inclination to generalize about the "plight" of native people, despite their cultural and geographic differences.

As for the Klamaths, they received little in federal funds to deal with alcoholism and other social problems when they lacked tribal status during termination. Then, restored as a federal tribe, Chairman Allen Foreman singled out a new drug and alcohol program for the treatment of young people. "We have two choices," he said. "We can continue with the status quo and continue to lose members to drugs and alcohol or we can all pitch in together to prevent tragedies from happening." As part of that effort, the Klamaths have been running treatment programs for members of all ages, at increasing levels of funding.

The Klamaths are now also receiving millions of dollars in federal funds each year for such programs as health-care as well as education, the care of

The Dependency Curse

children, prevention of family violence, support for adoptions, distribution of food and expansion of housing. These programs probably had much to do with attracting the return of more than 1,000 natives who had dispersed during termination. Further, the tribe has lowered the blood requirement for membership, adding to the tribal population and making more natives eligible to receive federal benefits.

If you visit the impressive tribal headquarters in Chiloquin, you'll see another big benefit from the restoration of the tribe: Employment. Tribal government, the small nearby casino and the federally funded programs provide 250 jobs.[12] But it is not nearly enough. Mario Sampson lists more jobs as the biggest need for the tribe. In fact, critics contend that the real purpose of the replacement of tribal leaders was to gain control of what jobs are available. Tellingly, newly elected tribal chairman Gary Frost is the husband of Roberta Frost, one of three women who staged a recall of previous leaders. But aside from the possibility of nepotism, there was another major reason for the recall campaign: tribal dissatisfaction had grown out of a tightening of federal funds, leading to cuts in benefits and services. "The BIA (Bureau of Indian Affairs) funds are decreasing, and the client caseload (welfare) is increasing," noted a budget report.

Meantime, the Klamaths have brought about little economic development to improve their finances in the 25 years since they reacquired status as an "independent" sovereign nation (a contradiction since they are still dependent on federal support.) Their lack of progress on development is not necessarily from lack of trying. Scholar Tom Trulove, a perceptive student of the Klamaths, contends it is unrealistic to expect much economic development in rural areas, such as the Klamath reservation, because markets, trained labor forces and other inputs "are simply not there and never will be." Of course, now the reservation barely exists, its size reduced from 800,000 acres to 300 acres, along with many cemeteries that mark so many premature deaths (and a people without jobs or hope?).

On the positive side, the tribe has completed a travel-center gateway to the wondrous Crater Lake National Park, is seeking to buy back land and is working to build other businesses, including wood processing operations on

VI. Klamaths Today

a "green enterprise park."[13] But Foreman pointed out more than a decade ago, when he was chairman, that the Klamaths were 13 years behind in producing a viable economic self-sufficiency plan required by their restoration law. They still don't have a plan acceptable to the federal government, partly because the government won't approve their long-standing goal of regaining their reservation. So after 25 years, true independence as a "nation" remained a dream, maybe partly because they have put so much of their effort into what seems impossible, getting back the reservation they sold (under duress?) for a huge profit.

A review of the two self-sufficiency plans, in 1992 and 2000, shows that the Klamaths were adamant for more than a decade in demanding the return of their land. The first plan cited dire social problems, blaming them on the loss of those lands. (A reality check is in order here: the social problems persisted long before the government bought their land, and continued at the end of termination.) The 1992 plan said plainly, "Former reservation lands must be returned...The tribes have not enjoyed full well-being and prosperity since their land was taken away...The tribes remain...convinced that full recovery cannot occur until land and people are reunited."[14] The next plan, in 2002, was no less demanding: "We must regain all federally owned former reservation lands. The land is the key not only for the economic survival of the tribes, but also for the mental, physical and spiritual health for all members of the Klamath, Modoc and Yahooskin Band of Snake Indians."[15]

As you would expect, the effort by the Klamaths to regain their land is not universally accepted. A handful of locals, as the tribal newsletter described them, were opposed to giving back even part of the original reservation. "Why should the taxpayers foot the bill to buy land to establish a separate country for the Klamath tribes?" wrote a group calling itself the Klamath Basin Alliance. "Isn't this fostering separatism, apartheid and racism?"

By then, in 2008, the Klamaths apparently had recognized the futility of trying to get back their entire 800,000-acre reservation and announced plans to buy back a 90,000-acre tract of timberland, the Mazama Forest, which they would restore and manage. As tribal leaders saw it, the land purchase would provide a cornerstone for their lagging economic development efforts. A spokesman for the land owner, the national conservation organization Trust for Public Lands, said that recovery of the land would be a "major achievement in their long struggle back to cultural independence and economic self-reliance." Added Joe Kirk, in the Klamath tribal newspaper, the land would not only provide the tribe with financial stability, but "is a significant part of our spiritual and cultural identity."

To pursue their goals, the Klamaths financed a feasibility study to look at a variety of possible projects: a biomass power plant, operations to process small diameter posts and poles, whole log wood chips and wood shavings, along with tribal logging to complement pre-commercial thinning of the forest by tribe's' new restoration crew. A well-respected planning and consultant firm found all the possible businesses to be feasible, said the tribe. (Consultants tend to tell the sponsors of their studies what they want to hear.)

Alas, such was not to be, for years. The tribe proposed to take over the Mazama Forest the next year, in 2009, and develop the forest-based enterprises in a newly-acquired industrial park at an old mill site. The sad fact is that more than six years later the proposal was still only a plan. What happened? The answer is two-fold: Lack of money and unrealistic expectations. For money, the tribe has hoped to get $21 million from the Klamath Basin Water Restoration Agreement, which was designed to settle a fight for scarce water among farmers, fishermen and three Indian tribes. But the agreement, requiring the approval of Congress, was stalled because of its $800 million cost. U.S. Senator Ron Wyden, a liberal Democrat, not a conservative Tea Party type, said in 2013 that the agreement, which included the Klamath land payment, was too expensive considering federal budget constraints.[16]

As for unrealistic expectations, the question could be asked, is the potential of the Mazama Forest so great as to provide the "financial stability" promised by Chairman Kirk? (A later chairman, Don Gentry, reiterated that promise.) The answer: Not necessarily. That was the conclusion of an analysis of the land proposal in the Journal of Political Ecology. Authors Kelly,

VI. Klamaths Today

Bliss and Gosnell pointed out that up to 80 percent of its valuable Ponderosa pine had been harvested in the 1930s, leaving a large supply of small lodgepole pine of little commercial value. Not only that, development of the Mazama property, isolated on the northwest corner of the former reservation, was facing a vastly diminished market for forest products in the region. And most important of all, the authors said, there may be a legitimate question whether the Klamaths had the capacity to restore the Mazama Forest. (Interestingly, the record doesn't show Klamaths opposing, early on, the heavy harvesting of reservation timber, which wiped out most of the value of the Mazama tract. To the contrary, a group of Klamaths wanted the government to cut and sell all the timber on their territory for their own cash payments from the revenue.)

The authors of the journal analysis summarized the problems of the proposed Mazama purchase thusly: Degraded timber conditions and a declining timber industry in the region made the purchase less than promising.[17]

While plans to buy the Mazama tract languished, the Klamaths announced an intent to purchase 385 acres of land south of Portland for manufacturing, retail or services development. Tribal chairman Joe Kirk told Klamaths it would provide jobs for the 500 members living in that area, far removed from the reservation. No, he said, it would not be used for a casino to lure Portland gamblers. But the representative of another tribe that operates a casino in the area was suspicious out of concern about competition, calling it "reservation shopping" (implying that the Klamaths would later build a casino on the satellite reservation site.)[18]

Not long after he spoke of the prospects of the land purchases, Kirk had been ousted as chairman by long-time tribal member Gary Frost, who instead of talking about economic development, expressed the desire to unify the Klamath tribes, then riven by internal conflict as they have been through much of their recent history.[19] Three years later, Don Gentry, a tribal official, was elected chairman pledging to represent a diversity of views in the Klamaths. Dealing with their welfare dependency was not on the announced agenda.

The Dependency Curse

While Frost preached unity, his election reflected the disunity of the Klamaths, as shown not only by the recall campaign that led to his victory, but also by oft-renewed efforts of a group of Modoc Indians (Frost is part Modoc) to withdraw from the Klamath tribe, citing 146 years of oppression as a "captive people," as well as the failure to achieve much economic development. Their goal, as a Modoc nation, said spokesman Perry Chesnut, is to become completely self-sufficient in 15 years and end any reliance on federal funding. "We want to be independent," he told the Herald and News of Klamath Falls. "We don't mind working for what we get."[20]

Lynn Schonchin, also part Modoc, says it's ludicrous for them to think they can get land and money as a separate tribe. He predicted a failure in the effort, just as the Klamath tribe has failed to get back its land. Certainly Schonchin has good reason to make those assessments.

As a retired history teacher, he knows about the ebb and flow of tribes and nations, including the long-ago suppression of his Modoc tribe. In fact, he gets strength from what his ancestors did to fight for the Modoc homes and families, even though they lost their fight. And he marvels at the hypocrisy of white ranchers when they complain about the quest for Indian fishing rights while they have the benefit of grazing their cattle on government land. Yes, Schonchin says he is irritated at times about these matters, but after overcoming a gambling addiction, he is more worried about his dependence on smoking, about a heart attack and terrible blood circulation in his legs.

Schonchin's story is worth telling in detail but it shows the ups and downs of the person, of successes and of personal problems (don't we all know of that?). He was chairman of the Klamaths three times, before and after termination, making him obviously part of the leadership class. Then he rose to be general manager, while serving as teacher and counselor at the Chiloquin high school. Married with children, he was a success in many ways, until the tribal casino, too small to be of much benefit to tribal members, was enough of a lure to make a dependent of Lynn Schonchin, cost him his job and prompted him to leave his wife of 42 years ("a great woman," he says now).

VI. Klamaths Today

After two years as manager of the tribe (this writer had interviewed him way back then), Schonchin was fired for using $2,000 of tribal money for his gambling. Tribal members isolated him; his wife tried to help him but he rejected her. "I don't know what happened," he says. "I fell apart." But he has recovered from his gambling addiction, repaid the money, ran the tribal drug treatment program for a while, and now in his late 60s, lives with a daughter and her five children, helping them "know who they are and who they want to be."

Schonchin knows who he is, a rebel deep down who grew long hair in defiance of school authorities, a descendent of "patriot" Schonchin John, leader of a rebellion in the late 1800s of Modoc Indians, who fought off the U.S. Army for many months in a futile effort to keep their homeland. Four of them, including Schonchin John, were executed for their participation in what were killings on both sides. (Also executed was Captain Jack, leader of the Modoc rebels; one of his descendants is Tom Ball, who became chairman of the Klamath Tribes, which includes the Modocs.) The U.S. government back then was the enemy, forcing Modoc and Yahooskin natives to live on the Klamath reservation as one nation under government control. For all his working life, Lynn Schonchin was part of that as a teacher, seeing the successes and, often, failures of native children. For all the failures, he is positive about the future because he has faith in younger people working for the tribe, who come to ask him about tribal culture and history.

Still, Schonchin is concerned about the future for the Klamaths; sees little hope that the tribe will regain its timber resource, and frets about the prospect of "massive cuts" in government funding. Unemployment already is high, he says, and is "going to get worse."

Like many Klamaths, Schonchin blames termination for many of the problems of the tribe. Another is scholar Bettles, also a tribal insider, now living in Eugene north of the reservation. He says the trauma of termination divided and dispersed tribal members. In the aftermath, he adds, "politics" and family rivalries have kept them from reuniting. If the "tribe" is riven by rivalries, it's not surprising in a population in which so many different tribes are represented, many through intermarriage. Only a small minority are full-blooded Klamaths. Lynn Schonchin is Klamath, Modoc, Paiute, Pit River and Shasta; his former wife, half Mexican. Joe Skahan, son of Klamath historian Barbara Alatorre, is an enrolled member of the Yakimas, his father's tribe.

Bettles, who fittingly was cultural resources director for the tribe, is Klamath, Nez Perce, Cauyuse and Warm Springs. It is worth noting again that the U.S. Army used Warm Springs Indians as scouts in their war against the Modocs. Lynn Schonchin's tribal ancestry. In this mix of tribes within the Klamaths, Bettles says there will always be nepotism—the favoring of family members in jobs, for example—because members are so interrelated. "When I was cultural director I did not have any immediate family, but I was related to almost everybody in my department," he says. (The plethora of tribes, and their mixing through intermarriage of natives and whites, challenges the concept of the "Indian," just as similar mixing makes it difficult for blacks, Jews, Latinos and Asians to identify themselves as one or another. More than half the Jewish people, for example, cross their religious line to marry.)

For all the differences, Bettles says outsiders don't understand how deep is the loyalty to the Klamath tribes, even though many, including his family, no longer live on the reservation. That's why he sees the need for them to come together as a "solid tribe" to develop a stronger economy based on small businesses. The Warm Springs Indians of Oregon, part of his heritage, are more prosperous because they still have a forest resource as well as a resort business, along with their casino. The Klamaths no longer have their forest or any major businesses, and thus many rely on government aid. Bettles does not. Still, for all of his personal successes, with his tribe and on his own, Bettles says, "We've had our ups and downs; I have tried to stay on the upside."

While Bettles now makes it on his own, his tribe does not. The Klamaths, a tribe of fewer than 4,000 members, have received almost $40 million in revenue over a 10-year period, most of it from the federal government to support the health and social programs, as well as to run their tribal government. The question for small tribes like the Klamaths, as raised by tribal

VI. Klamaths Today

elder Schonchin, is how long they can continue to receive so much federal money in the face of the large national deficit. Congress showed during termination that it could cut off such funding despite the tribal claim that age-old treaties gave them the right, as independent sovereign nations, to such special treatment. Cutbacks in federal spending have already squeezed Klamath finances.

Meantime, there is little evidence that the federal funding is helping the Klamaths overcome the alcoholism, drug use, premature deaths and other social problems that continue unabated, with limited exceptions. In fact, Schonchin says that alcoholism among Klamath young people seems to be on the rise again, after receding for a while.

If dependency—there's that word again—helps account for the intractable nature of this profound social pathology of the Klamaths and most Native Americans, what can or should be done to reduce the reliance on the government or the free money of casino gambling? Without any change in the present situation, natives are answering by continuing to migrate to the cities, thus diminishing the concentration of poverty and its attendant problems on the reservations, the "red apartheid" of reservation segregation, as critics call it?

For sure, heaping more pity on the natives, as is done periodically by the news media (see recent New York Times accounts of drunkenness at a reservation in South Dakota and widespread rapes of native women at a reservation in North Dakota), won't bring about change. And politically, the natives are too tiny a population (at 5.2 million; less than 2 percent of the American total) to exert much pressure for reform in government programs. If the history of socio-economic reform is any guide, the push for change must come from within the 560 tribes. Barbara Alatorre's sons call for education and jobs (and more casino revenue). Maybe the seeds of change have already been planted in the education of Klamaths like Tom Ball and Gordon Bettles and the graduates of an expanding tribal education system. Or maybe a movement for change will grow in the tribes from the natives who are expressing concerns about the supposed effects of a dependency culture. Or from the casino money used for constructive purposes.

The Dependency Curse

Many other Klamaths also surmount obstacles to make it in life, often partly out of self-interest, which can be a powerful motivating force. Ball notes that some Klamaths move to where they can get a job and come back to visit. "We see a lot of that," he says. Members of Alatorre's extended family moved to Portland to take advantage of job training provided by the federal government during termination. (But she also helped set up meetings of Klamaths members in Portland to maintain tribal ties and push for reforms.) In some ways, termination of timber-sale payments for the Klamaths was similar to the phased termination of welfare for all Americans. In both cases, some people suffered from it; others became more self-reliant—out of self-interest.

On a tribal level, it certainly was self-interest that caused some of the Klamaths to push for increased timber sales earlier in the last century to boost payments to members, and then, when they no longer owned the timber, to oppose sales as a claimed threat to their hunting and fishing rights.

On a national level, for all the romantic talk of native devotion to nature and the land, it was self-interest that prompted early tribal people, in order to survive, to wipe out vegetation where they lived in the arid southwest, and then to move on to other areas where they would do the same. It was self-interest for Indians to slaughter buffalo for their tongues, which they considered a delicacy. It also was self-interest that led the Ojibway to fight the Sioux for territory in the northern plains, before the intrusion of white settlers. And, finally, it was self-interest that prompted the Europeans to push out the natives to clear the way for farmers, miners and other newcomers.

Meantime, tribal loyalists like Ball emphasize the strengths of the natives and speak optimistically of the future. Says Ball, "We have been here forever and we will be here forever." (Well, been here 12,000 years or so.)

CHAPTER VII

Conclusion

WHAT CONCLUSION can be drawn from this account of two Native American tribes, the Klamaths of Oregon and the Shakopee Mdewakanton Sioux of Minnesota? What conclusion not just as related to these two tribes, but as applied to most other original Americans? In fact, the best conclusion may well be that there is no conclusion. That was the opinion of journalist Roberta Ulrich, a leading author on native affairs, when I asked her to do a critique of my work. "It's obvious that you believe strongly that dependency is the root of all evil for tribes," she wrote. "However, I don't think you have fully made your case. I see more of the other issues you touch on as equally related to tribal problems."

Yes, author Ulrich, I agree that I have not fully made my case for dependency as the root cause of native problems. I have presented the possibility that it is a major cause of these problems, but I can't prove it, any more than anyone can prove the cause of a pervasive alcoholism, or of high unemployment and low educational achievement, or of so many dysfunctional families. Is a genetic component a factor, or is it situational in the poverty of "ghetto" life on many of the reservations? No one has proved that these or any other factors are the cause of the "native problem." It may be that they all contribute to the intractable problem. And I have made a case, as propounded by native leaders and journalists, that dependency is part of the problem.

But some conclusions can be drawn from the experience of native people. One is their resilience, their refusal to give up their identity as descendants of the first settlers of this nation. The other is their loyalty to that tribal heritage, whether living on so-called reservations established by the government, or the two-thirds who have migrated to the cities by compulsion or by free choice. And the third conclusion, propounded not originally by me, but by some native leaders and journalists, is that they suffer from the deleterious effects of a continuing dependency on the government or, for the Sioux and other tribes, a dependence on casino gambling wealth.

Of course, this bottom-line conclusion is open to challenge. Any writer has to concede, in reviewing a group of people that has been studied and written about perhaps more than any other, that it is risky to come to any firm conclusions about two or two hundred tribes of Native Americans. The best that can be done, perhaps, is to reject the stereotypes that have been applied to these two tribes, and all tribes. These stereotypes treat these original Americans as outsiders, the other people, when they should be considered as we descendants of immigrants accept ourselves, subject to all the conflicts and the cooperation, loves and hatreds, selfishness and generosity, peacemaking and warmongering, goodness and badness, and all the rest of the human condition. This writer has seen much of it in his multiracial family of eight children, along with 11 grandchildren and assorted partners. What a surprise!

But there is more to Ulrich's exceedingly honest critique of my work. "It seems that most of the people you interviewed escaped the ill effects of dependency," she wrote. "If dependency is so pervasively evil, why didn't it affect them? And why were others unable to escape? (Are there clues in Appalachia or in big-city ghettos? I don't know.) My suspicious is that it has a lot to do with being able to see the possibility of some other way and that may come from parents, teacher, reading." Indeed, those circumstances could explain the successes of some of the natives I cited in my narrative. My

VII. Conclusion

initial response, that some people do rise above adverse circumstances, was glib and hardly persuasive.

Continuing her critique, Ulrich asks whether racism, rather than the social pathology I emphasized, has played a part in Indian unemployment. Again, I was somewhat dismissive, answering, "racism certainly is a big factor in unemployment of blacks, but I'm not sure it is a compelling issue for natives. Lack of job skills, because they do not have a work history, could be more important." Ulrich didn't buy my answer in whole, saying "…in the era before and during termination there was as much prejudice against Indians in some areas as there was against blacks…This was very true around the Yakama (then Yakima) and Nez Perce reservations. I remember as a child being in Lewiston, Idaho, with my mother eating at a restaurant with a sign 'we reserve the right to refuse service to anyone.' I asked her what that meant. She stumbled around a lot before explaining it meant "no Indians."' (And for sure no jobs in those restaurants.)

Racism, of course, played no part in the difficulties of the early Klamaths, the main focus of this commentary. As we have reported in detail, the Klamaths survived as a primitive people on the fruit of the land. But this was not the idyllic existence, living off what nature had to offer, as some writers have portrayed Indian life prior to the "invasion" of white Europeans. Nature did not protect them from hunger in drought years or keep them warm in the bitter cold winters of their high-altitude domain. It could have been worse, however, except for one major change: The introduction of the horse.

In fact, in one of the great ironies of native American history, it was the white Europeans (Spanish) who brought horses to America, which the natives used in many ways, for good and ill. Many tribes used them for attacks on the white settlers who were invading their lands. The imperial Sioux, ancestors of the Shakopee Mdewakanton Sioux, used them to push aside rival tribes and create a large empire in the Midwest. The Klamaths as well used their horses for raids on other tribes, sometimes taking slaves to, yes, trade for more horses. And let's not forget that these horses were indispensable for the Modocs of Oregon and the Sioux of Minnesota, as well as

The Dependency Curse

many other tribes, in wars against the government to retain their tribal lands.

As you can see, and as we have noted, the history of Native Americans is not a simple-minded account of good (natives) versus bad (Europeans). In this version of events, the government wasn't all bad either. The government assigned the Klamaths to a reservation in the mid-1960s not just to clear the way for European settlers and protect them from marauding attacks by the natives, but also to protect the Klamaths from attacks by the European settlers. (That's one version of those events; one this author accepts.) At least on the reservation the Klamaths remained on their homeland, received supplies and annuities from the government in the early reservation years, and in the early 1900s began receiving substantial monthly payments from the sales of their timber. It was enough for them to live on, supplemented for some by part-time jobs. Then the government, challenging their status as sovereign nations, took over their forest assets and gave them a substantial payment for it, while eliminating their privileged status as a tribe. For various reasons, this was not the answer to their problems; prompting them to win back their tribal standing in the late 1900s and to receive all the benefits again as dependent sovereign nations under government sanction. As we have noted, however, the social problems—a social pathology as a native scholar put it—persist today whether the Klamaths remain in or near their diminished reservation—barely more than 300 acres of scattered parcels—or in the cities to which more than half have migrated. (of 3,673 Klamaths, 2,000 have gone elsewhere).[1] And through all of this, they remained a dependent people, dependent on timber sales and on the one-time fortune from the takeover of their forest resource, and again on the government. Yes, that dependency continues to this day, a dependency again on the government, back where they started on their reservation. A dependency on free money and benefits, without having to work for them. A dependency that could be at the root of the social pathology.

Before setting forth any conclusions about the ever-existing dependency, we should examine how a relatively new federal policy has or has not reduced this government domination and tribal dependency in the use of

VII. Conclusion

government money. That policy was proposed in 1961 by a group of young natives, college graduates, at a conference in Chicago, then espoused by President Lyndon Johnson in 1968. At that time the policy was to "encourage" self-determination by native people in the handling of the government largess.[2] Then, in a startling special message to Congress in 1970, the sometimes-liberal President Richard Nixon proposed that Congress should empower tribes to actually take over control of federal programs, to run a health clinic, build a community center, set up day care programs, write an economic development plan. The tribes would receive federal money directly and run the programs themselves. Congress enacted his proposals just five years later. It was official, embedded in law.[3]

But it was not universally endorsed by native leaders, according to one account two decades later. "The administration of federal programs gave tribal councils the experience and self-confidence to demand even greater self-government," wrote author James Rawls in a well-documented history of Native Americans. "Some leaders complained, however, that the flow of federal funds was undercutting the movement toward tribal independence. Native American communities, they argued, were becoming more dependent than ever on the federal government." As they saw it, tribal governments were becoming more administrators of government programs than tribal governments, more concerned about funding for those programs than about developing comprehensive plans for sustained growth.[4]

Now, in almost 40 years since self-determination was enacted into law, President Barack Obama's newly appointed Secretary of Interior told delegates to the National Congress of American Indians that she, Sally Jewell, would work with tribes "nation-to-nation" to protect their sovereignty and become more economically independent. She received a standing ovation.[5]

Okay, it still sounds good, but has this policy, as now enunciated, substantially altered the dependency of Native Americans? On the contrary, it can be argued, as we have noted, that it has added to the problems of tribal people. In the latest critique of the policy, as a U.S. Senate investigative report saw it in 1989: "By allowing tribal officials to handle hundreds of millions in federal funds without stringent criminal laws or adequate enforcement, Congress has left the American Indian people vulnerable to corruption." A decade later, the late native journalist Bill Lawrence in Minnesota contended that tribal sovereign immunity, upon which self-determination is based, was by that time "the single biggest factor" contributing to corruption and discord on American Indian reservations because it led to a lack of accountability.[6]

Lawrence cited examples of the corruption in Minnesota, including felony convictions of six tribal officials. He concluded, "It is time to end the Noble Savage Mentality that keeps tribes in the ambiguous position of being both wards of the federal government and supposed sovereign nations. We should be nothing other than full U.S. citizens with all the rights, responsibilities and protections thereof."The problem, in short, was that under the policy of self-determination, native leaders could act without the democratic controls imposed on the general population. Economist Tom Trulove noted "the difficulties in squaring ethnically based sovereignty with principles of democracy and equal citizenship."

In one of the most noxious examples of tribal corruption in Minnesota, home of the Mystic Lake millionaires, chief Darrell Wadena of the White Earth tribe got more than $400,000 from a secret interest in a tribal member's drywall firm doing work on the tribe's casino. Conflicts of interest? The rules didn't apply on semi-sovereign Indian reservations, said Wadena. He went to prison anyway, convicted of conspiracy, bribery, money laundering, theft and embezzlement. The jury that convicted him decided that the "rules" did apply. Before his death at age 75, Wadena spent his final years running bingo concessions at the casino that he had built and that led to his undoing.[7]

In the nation, federal audits have found that American Indian tribes misappropriate tens of millions of taxpayer dollars, using the money to pay utility bills and mortgages, for horses and ATVs, personal shopping trips or for gambling at tribal casinos. According to a story by the Associated Press, a former inspector general blamed the abuses on a reluctance by the government to "take on the tribes," rather "to make nice…to be their friends." It's a patronizing stance that deprives tribes of money that should be used for

VII. Conclusion

legitimate programs.[8] (Well, it must be said that the U.S. government, because it didn't trust native tribes to manage their resources, had to repay billions of dollars for its own mismanagement of the tribal accounts.)

To their credit, neither the Klamaths of Oregon nor the Shakopee Sioux of Minnesota have been corrupted by self-determination. No criminal cases have been brought against either one, contrary to the convictions cited by the outspoken Lawrence in other Minnesota tribes. The problem for the Klamaths is not inbred corruption, but the fact that self-determination hasn't helped them at all in becoming self-sufficient as a so-called sovereign nation. The reason, as we have observed, is that since termination paid them for their forest they have lacked the resources to do so. So far, they have built a casino remote from the gambling public and lacking a hotel to make it a destination attraction. They' also have a small visitor center for the nearby Crater Lake National Park. Beyond that, the roughly $4 million in "self-determination" money received in a recent year (a third of the $14 million in federal funds given to the Klamaths for various programs), supports most of the programs needed by any community of Americans.

For the 1,670 Klamaths still living on or near the reservation, the money also supports a bureaucracy that hires consultants to churn out development plans, mostly based on their futile effort to get back their land. The money also makes it possible to retain attorneys to get the most possible out of the government for the loss of that land. That bureaucracy operates out of an attractive tribal government building, produces a newspaper to keep members at home and away informed on issues, thrives on countless meetings and endures the political conflict over who will run their government and control the government jobs. It's a viable government, subject to the votes of the people, running a host of programs, but it is still dependent on the federal government, almost three decades after regaining tribal "sovereignty."

As for the Shakopee Sioux, after an early battle for control of the tribe, tribal leaders have avoided challenge by spending millions to buy off competition and maintain their gambling monopoly. They also have won the favor of other tribes by contributing millions more to meet their needs. The Sioux have plenty of millions in casino wealth to do all that.

The Dependency Curse

What will it take for the Klamaths and other tribes to make themselves into truly self-supporting sovereign nations? Researchers Stephen Cornell and Joseph P. Kalt at the Harvard Project on American Indian Economic Development and the Native Nations Institution at the University of Arizona make it sound not too hard. Shaping their futures, they write, "will require not simply the assertion of sovereignty—a claim to rights and power—it will require the effective exercise of that sovereignty. The task tribes face is to use the power they have to build viable nations before the opportunity slips away. This is the major challenge facing Indian country today. It also is the key to solving the seemingly intractable problem of reservation poverty. Sovereignty, nation-building and economic development go hand in hand. Without sovereignty and nation-building, economic development is likely to remain a frustratingly elusive dream."[9]

Lots of words there. But the researchers don't address the seminal question: how long will the Indian tribes, like the Klamaths, be able to rely on the government to assist them in building "viable nations." Or even should they continue to count on the government? As pointed out in this narrative, some native activists have warned that this dependence on the government—and casino wealth—can't last forever. Moreover, despite the financial support that the government has granted in return for treaty rights to much of their land, the government can terminate those rights, with compensation as it did for the Klamaths, or reduce government support as it has done for all tribes at times of over-all fiscal restraint, regardless of native claims of sovereignty as nations. For example, the administration of the revered (by many) President Ronald Reagan substantially cut back federal funding of native health and education programs in the early 1980s.[10]

Scott Kayla Morrison, an attorney and Choctaw tribal member, takes on the claim that "our land was stolen and the federal government owes us." She asks, when will the debt be paid? In two centuries, she notes, the government had shelled out $52 billion for their land and for tribal support. "No other race has been compensated to such an extent, and no other race expects to be supported by the federal government in perpetuity. It would cost less to send every Indian in the country to college."[11] But many

VII. Conclusion

advocates within the native nations do expect to be supported indefinitely as a form of reparation for their land losses, as guaranteed under treaties of the 1800s.

It should be pointed out that African American advocates have gotten nowhere in their demands for reparations for their forced relocation and servitude. As recently as 2013, 14 Caribbean nations demanded reparations from their former colonial rulers, namely Britain, France and the Netherlands.[12] Likewise, it is worth observing that many nations, including native nations, have never been reimbursed for territories lost in intertribal wars or because of wars and invasions by outside forces, World War I and WW II being prime examples. (This author was struck by a report about the horrifying lynching of thousands of black Americans to enforce segregation after slavery was ended. That use of terrorism was far worse than anything the white Europeans did to original Americans during that time.) As for the descendants of African slaves in the Americas, they know that the Native Americans enjoy the benefits of perpetual reparations, while they get nothing.

My wife and I learned more about all this when we visited St. Kitts, Dominica, Martinque and Antiua in the southern Caribbean. We learned about this legacy of slavery, as one writer put it, gaining perspective and context for the Native American experiences. It was a sort of travelogue in inhumanity, combined with our trips past many of the native enclaves in this country, all described throughout this narrative. We saw the tiny shacks of the people of Antique, worse than the rundown houses of the Crow Indians of Montana, even as 15,000 people, reeking of affluence, emerged from the monster cruise ships nearby to buy jewelry, watches and perfumes. We read that British soldiers massacred 2,000 Carib natives, two years after a British ship captain had made peace with them.

A consideration of this past and present make it difficult to assess who is entitled to what in redress for the inhumanity of our species. Remember that the Sioux once "controlled" one-fifth of the country, acquired through conquest of other tribes, sometimes through the massacre of rivals. Could they claim the right to that land? Or could the 3,700 Klamaths claim the

The Dependency Curse

right to freely roam over the 22 millon acres of territory they once "controlled," using the latter term loosely. It's true that the government paid for the takeover of most of that land, but no payment would be adequate to cover the worth of such a big chunk of the country.

Attorney Morrison, meantime, did not mention another native dependence, that is, dependence for many on alcohol, the well identified scourge of native life. White traders helped create that dependence in earlier centuries as a way to exploit their trade for animal pelts and other products. As author White put it, liquor "created unlimited demand and allowed whites to dictate the forms of exchange."[13] While the American colonists also were heavy drinkers, they didn't allow it to undermine their society as it did the natives.

In one notable case today, liquor companies use that dependence to make millions of dollars a year from beer sales to members of the Pine Ridge reservation in South Dakota, all from a nearby Nebraska town of 22 residents and four buildings, known as White Clay. Retired Judge James Randall, a long-time champion of native causes and fierce critic of their dependence, described the situation thusly: "The existence of White Clay, as a liquor cartel, is a crushing blow to the Oglala Sioux." He added that the tax money Nebraska derives from beer sales to Sioux is "blood money. Money soaked in alcoholism, other drug abuse, liquor sales to minors, car wrecks with bleeding, maimed and dead (victims), brutal beatings, brutal stabbings and a history of violent homicides."[14] In the quirky sense of humor shown by some natives, one writer described death from alcoholism as death by natural causes.[15]

While alcohol has also been a problem for the Klamaths (and maybe for the Sioux), it is only part of a dependence culture, a dependence they chose in the last century. The Klamaths fought to regain government support after almost three decades of independence upon being paid for their land in the early 1960s. The small Sioux band had been cast adrift after an uprising against the government. But they insisted on dependence on that government and got it more than 100 years later. At that time, in 1969, they were granted tribal status and were given a small tract of land for having sided

VII. Conclusion

with the government in the Sioux war. Then they switched from that dependence to a dependence on casino gambling.

Cornell and Kalt do cite tribes, including Morrison's Choctaws, that have broken from the prevailing pattern of social pathology without depending on gaming: The Mississippi Choctaws are one of the largest employers in their state; the White Mountain Apaches have made forest products, skiing, recreation and other enterprises into the economic anchor of east-central Arizona, and the Salish and Kootenai tribes in Montana have built a successful economy based on tourism, agriculture and retail services. "These activities," they write, "reduce the support burdens on the rest of society—on taxpayers—and reduce the squandering of human resources that has plagued Indian country for more than a century."[16] Some casino tribes have wisely diversified their economies by investing gambling profits in hotels and other income-producing properties.

The Klamaths have been trying, as a dependent "sovereign nation," to become self-sufficient since they were restored in 1986 as a federally recognized tribe. Are they succeeding? In economic development the answer is no. In personal achievement, no also. I'll repeat for emphasis that the tribe has created only a couple of job-producing enterprises, one being its small casino.

I'll also repeat for emphasis what Klamath tribal insiders are saying about their continuing social problems: people cashing their welfare checks and buying beer all day, or dealing drugs out of their homes, drinking alcohol until they are "out of their minds," failing with impunity to do their tribal jobs, going to tribal meetings only for a free lunch, perpetuating prejudice and divisions within the tribe.

The late tribal chairman Seldon Kirk was right in his long-ago lament about the ill effects of dependency. On the other hand, the Shakopee Sioux in Minnesota are prospering from their dependence on their huge casino, but a chairman of that tribe also has complained about how that dependency is warping the lives of their young people. Half don't graduate from high school and an abysmally low percentage of them go on to college. But, oh yes, they have expensive cars and live in big houses for a distorted version of the American dream.[17]

The Dependency Curse

Maybe extravagant wealth, however, is not all bad, just somewhat bad. The social problems of the Klamaths and the Sioux, are relatively minor compared with the problems depicted in stories about other natives across the country: the suicides among young people, crimes against children and women, endemic alcoholism and the over-all poverty, worst of any group of Americans. Then there are natives victimizing natives, such as two tribes, asserting tribal sovereignty, charging allegedly exorbitant interest on payday loans. Native scholar Gerald Vizenor decries an emphasis on this "victimry" in the Indian population, but in any fair and balanced treatment of the Indian people, an author must address these ailments as well as the many successes of the people.

In the face of this social pathology, the original Americans survive. They survive as an ethnic group despite their diversity in hundreds of reservations scattered around the country, despite their dispersal—two thirds of them—to the cities, despite their dependence primarily on the government they blame for many of their ills. This should not come as a surprise. Jewish, Irish, Asian, Roma and many other ethnic and religious people maintain their identity while enduring prejudice in years past and present wherever they live. The Jews, particularly, were a wandering people until they established a homeland in Israel, where many settle or visit. An estimated 11 million Roma, who came from India to Europe centuries ago, are now scattered across the continent, without a homeland.[18]

Native people have their reservation "homelands," to which many go back and forth from their city dwellings. More than that, some continue to be involved in tribal affairs or, at the least, keep abreast of tribal issues and activities. On a personal level, the author and his family enjoyed periodic visits to his one-time farm "homeland," crossing a creek and traipsing through the woods, where he spent many happy times as a child.

Some Klamaths decide later in life to be involved with tribal members. They can do so on a website described as a "gathering spot for Klamath, Modoc and Yahooskin Snake Paiute peoples." Consider this posting: "Hello, my name is Debra (Farmer) Rincon Lopez from Portland Oregon. I am Klamath tribal member. My mother is Barbara Alatorre (Farmer) who is the

VII. Conclusion

tribal historian for the Klamath tribes. She's our chief & has always been of our family too. I hope to learn about news & meet friends and relations I lost touch with in my past. I hope to be more involved in things in the future."[19]

Some Klamaths return to help their tribe or remain active after leaving. Scholar Tom Ball went back to do research for a doctorate and be elected chairman, then left to be an official at the University of Oregon, where he received his doctoral degree. He indirectly helped the Klamaths in setting up a university liaison program with native tribes. Ike Skelton spent a long time away in the Navy and at college, then went to Portland, but just couldn't stand it in the big city and returned home to work on a cultural program. After eight years as tribal chairman, Allen Foreman retired to run a nearby ranch but continued to serve on the tribal council. Alatorre, a central figure in this narrative, stayed in Portland, far away from the reservation, but continued to be involved In Klamath affairs as a relentless activist, volunteer historian, and honest critic of tribal leadership. As we have noted, two of her adult sons also live elsewhere and have successful careers, while continuing to follow tribal affairs; one is adamantly opposed to the dependency of some tribal members. Alatorre's offspring reflect the views of their mother.

"Let me begin by saying how proud I am to be a member of the Klamath tribe," she says. "…Our ancient predecessors had to adapt to changing conditions to survive drastic climate changes. A large area of the northwest had an ice glacier covering about 13,000 years ago. The ancients survived the conditions and we are still here today."

In some ways, native people live in two or more cultures, in their reservation homeland and in nearby cities or rural areas. It is difficult, however, to define culture for the natives in view of intermarriage with members of other tribes, Mexicans and European Americans. In fact, "culture" is whatever the individual decides is his or her dominant ethnicity, if any. Some individuals simply don't care, being too far removed from ethnic parentage or embodying too many genetic differences to bother with defining themselves in that way, or consider it irrelevant, as does this author of German, Swiss and Dutch background. One of this author's sons, Native

The Dependency Curse

American and African American, just calls himself an American (and a patriot), a good reflection of the characteristics of much of the population in this country.

At the same time, my spouse and I have seen first-hand the tug of ethnic and "cultural" identity in our extended family. A granddaughter, who is Jewish, complained that her university, from which she has graduated, lacked diversity in a student body that is more than two-thirds Jewish. (Her father and two uncles, married to our daughters, are Jewish.) At the same time she declared pride in being Jewish, partly a religious identity that includes people, like her, who are secular as well as super-religious to nationalities as disparate as countries of Europe, Morocco in the Middle East and, of all places, Ethiopia in Africa. Another granddaughter, who is Native-American, African-American and White-American, went to the southern states on a college trip commemorating the fight against Jim Crow segregation. That same year she went to the Pine Ridge Indian reservation in South Dakota as part of her college social-work program. She expresses pride in her western Yakima native racial heritage. (After reading a draft of this book, she instructed me to capitalize the "n" in Native American.)

Or consider this diversity: A nephew and niece of mine, gay and lesbian, hooked up in same-sex relationships with Native Americans, man and woman. The gay nephew, however, broke up with his partner, member of the Navaho tribe, because of conflict between the two. Their mother, my sister, has been deeply immersed in Native American cultures; as an artist, she painted a picture of our mother with a Native American look. A grandson, who is part Native American, had a girlfriend, also Native American, but they, too, broke up over conflict in their relationship. My, oh my, I should point out that this diversity and multiple identities do not dominate the lives of our family members; they have enough to deal with in the exigencies of everyday life. As do most Americans, however diverse.

Among the Klamaths, Lynn Schonchin, former tribal official living in the environs of the reservation, tells how he asserted his cultural tradition by wearing beads and letting his hair grow for braids at the public high school where he taught history. When a school authority asked "why I had hair so

VII. Conclusion

long, I said, 'because I can.' He also had trouble with me wearing beads. I told him he didn't do anything about teachers wearing Coca Cola T-shirts."

It is noteworthy that the Oglala Sioux natives, the same tribal family as the Shakopee band, make up the population at Pine Ridge. But that reservation, which severely suffers from alcoholism and early deaths, is one of the poorest in the country, while the Shakopee people are super-wealthy and well-managed. Why the difference? One is location. The Pine Ridge reservation, like the Klamaths' reserve, is located too far from any major population center to attract the droves of gamblers who patronize the Shakopee casino. Also like the Klamaths, it is situated on land poorly suited for agriculture, leaving many native farmers with a subsistence livelihood. Another is leadership. The Pine Ridge people have been poorly led at least part of the time. In the 1970s their controversial chairman Richard Wilson was accused of using a private militia to suppress political opponents.[20] The Shakopee Sioux, also a dirt-poor band, sought and gained dependence on government as an officially designated tribe in the 1960s, but then became the beneficiaries of astute leaders who saw the economic possibilities of gambling and exploited their location near the multi-million population of the Twin Cities to build an unequaled economy, independent of the government, but dependent on a human addiction.

The history of the larger Sioux nation, however, is far more complicated than any simplistic rendition of any tortured relationship with white Europeans. Starting in the 1700s, the powerful Chippewa Indians, not whites, fought the Sioux for 130 years and ultimately drove them out of their homelands in Minnesota and northern Wisconsin. The Sioux nation in turn fought other tribes to the south and west, eventually dominating a huge territory, one-fifth of the country.[21] Of course, that didn't last as the white settlers and miners, backed by the army, moved in to vie for the land. In the newly acquired territory, the Sioux went to a war against the army, under the brilliant leader Red Cloud, and after a short-lived and celebrated victory were defeated and forced by the government to live at Pine Ridge. Meantime, in southern Minnesota they were defeated in an uprising that had been marked by the killing of many settlers, for which 38 natives were executed.

The Dependency Curse

In both of these cases, there were enough barbaric atrocities on both sides to match the horrible conflicts of today in many parts of the world. (The Sioux warriors cut off the penises of victims and stuffed them in their mouths; some fighters in religious tribes in Iraq and Syria today have cut off the heads or even crucified adversaries.) In different ways, the Sioux, like the Modocs in Oregon, were reacting to threats against their livelihood. Thus the endless wars, then and now, between tribes and nations, in the interplay of the quest for domination or independence. As we have emphasized, there is little that is romantic about this tribal conflict, whether for the survivors of the 19th century "Indian wars" in America, or in the battles now between those religious tribes in the Middle East and Africa. This author uses the word "romantic" as often applied to the Native Americans, but It could be argued, and this author so argues, that "romantic" could well be removed from any discourse on native history considering the murder, massacres and slave-taking that native warriors perpetuated on each other in their tribal conflicts. (Chief Red Cloud was viewed as a great leader of the Sioux but one should not overlook the terrible atrocities he inflicted on other tribes in his quest for territory.) It's also hard to justify use of the word "romantic" in considering the profound, seemingly intractable social problems that beset the natives in the aftermath of their long-ago wars against the government.

As this author has said, resilience is a better word to describe why many native people have survived through wars, dependence, independence and back to dependence, however debilitating the latter may be (if it is). It's resilience as manifested by the Klamaths when, after the many long years of being a "non-tribe," the newly constituted tribe quickly did surveys to determine their needs and laid out plans, however futile so far, to achieve self-sufficiency. And most tellingly, it's a resilience as applied to Edison Chiloquin, who was remembered after he died a while ago for his heroics as an Army scout during World War II, his ability to discard alcoholism, his love for his extended family and, most of all, for his refusal to accept a $273,000 payment for his ancestral lands when tribal rights were terminated. That's how the Klamath Falls Herald & News described this man who lived all his life in the reservation town of Chiloquin, named after his

VII. Conclusion

great-grandfather Chief Chiloquin, this multi-dimensional man who produced paintings and pen and ink drawings, who with family and friends maintained a sacred fire at a village site. Sell his land? "It would be like selling part of you, or a part of our ancestors," he explained before his death at age 79. Allen Foreman, tribal chairman at the time of his memorial service, said of him, "He stood up for what he believed in." A former wife said his advice was "be strong. Don't walk, run. Don't sit down."[22]

Add persistence to resilience to explain why the native people survive despite adversity. Even after selling their homeland to the government, the Klamaths retained their tribal identity partly by waging and winning a court battle to maintain fishing rights on their former reservation. Other tribes fight in other ways to retain what they consider to be their rights. To the north in Washington state, Nisqually native Billy Frank Jr. got himself arrested 50 times in asserting his right to fish in "tribal" waters. As a writer with the Associated Press, this author covered one of those fish-ins in the 1960s, attending a late-night strategy meeting with actor Marlon Brando and native leaders prior to his arrest that they staged to dramatize their cause. Ultimately Frank prevailed when a federal judge upheld the fishing rights of his Nisqually tribe, transforming him from outlaw to voice of wisdom and authority, according to the New York Times. After he died at age 83 in 2014, President Obama hailed him for his courage and determination in fighting to preserve those centuries-old native rights.

As for Chiloquin, he made his protest by staying on his land. On the contrary, many Klamaths have gone to Portland for jobs, but they return regularly to their reservation homeland, just as Jews go to Israel, or the Irish go to Ireland. And they form nationality groups in the cities, as immigrants from other countries established "national" churches, Polish, Irish and German. And the natives like Alatorre keep fighting for the return of the land that once was theirs. She has led a group of Klamaths in Portland, as part of a mini-reservation, meeting regularly for friendships and to develop action plans or to complain about leaders who don't measure up. Sound familiar?

As could be expected, Klamaths are concerned about more than land return. Members at a recent meeting severely criticized management of the

The Dependency Curse

tribe's restaurant and casino. An employee of the casino was back on the job after being accused of sexual harassment; others appear for work looking slovenly; a casino board member went out to form an electrical company to do work on a deli and wanted to be paid for it. Then there was that $2 million loss on aborted plans to expand the casino, prompting a tribal member to say, "We have got to have business people on that board and not clowns." Some members called for removal of the board to save the $100 paid per meeting to each member. It was a pretty darn good example of American democracy at work, by descendants of some of the original Americans.[23]

And there are those other continuing problems. The nine cemeteries on tribal property are testimony to the premature deaths of many Klamaths. The many priorities listed in a recent issue of the Klamath News are testimony to the failure, after decades of effort, to shed the yoke of dependence on government. The priorities are among continuing challenges: economic development, protection of water rights, organizational structure, funding, culture, health and even morale. Interestingly, a Klamath News priority entry on reservation land recovery, that long-time goal, went this way: "Identified, but not enough time for thorough discussion." Of course, the issue has been discussed, over and over for 25 years. Regardless, a telling entry on a water rights negotiating team shows how the wheels of government keep spinning. There have been too many meetings to mention during a time from July through September. Yes, lots of meetings. And conferences to attend. Along with a power-point presentation now and then.

For all their failures in dealing with the many challenges and attaining true independence, the Klamaths can claim to have a well-functioning government, subject to the vote of the people, marked by peaceful transitions from one leadership to another, maintained in a classy government building, with a division of labor by function, with an extremely capable public information officer who produces a regular newspaper, with reports on meetings and finances available on racks in the main lobby, with government files readily produced on request. All of that was obvious to this journalist in a recent visit.

VII. Conclusion

What it all means is that this tribe and many others are not on the verge of extinction even though less than half them any longer live on a reservation, the others having joined in the great migration to the cities. On the contrary, tribal enrollments are way up as thousands of natives reclaim identity and culture and seek government benefits. Even if they live in cities Indians are eligible for health, job and other services. The increase in the native population also is a reflection of a worldwide resurgence of nationhood, as shown in a rising nationalism at the same time economic "globalism" obscures national boundaries. The tiny island countries in the Caribbean aren't giving up their nationhood. Nor is the even smaller, 65-member, Suquamish tribe on an island off Seattle, Washington.

The issue for the remote tribes like the Klamaths, with little or no resources or prospects for any major economic development, is how long can they count on the federal government to prop them up, with millions of dollars per year. In perpetuity? Not necessarily, as shown by cutbacks in support from time to time, despite claimed treaty rights established more than a century ago. For the tribes with revenue from coal, oil or casinos, the glory ride can continue until the resources are depleted and the casinos suffer from the competition of a national gambling mania. (Like casinos, Big Oil isn't always the final answer for tribal ills, causing corruption as it does in other oil-rich nations of the world.)

Gambling mania? You bet. As native tribes clamor for cash from casinos, some states are doing the same, despite indications that the betting business may be on the wane. New York state has been considering options for four casino operations, including a billion-dollar gambling proposal near Manhattan, even as four casinos have closed in nearby Atlantic City. Interestingly, the proposed developer of the project near Manhattan was the Malaysian conglomerate Genting Group, which financed the Foxwoods casino for the Pequot native tribe in Connecticut almost three decades ago. As if a harbinger, as I have noted, the Pequots recently had to cut off casino payments to tribal members, and force some of them to turn to food shelves, because it created too much debt in an overly ambitious expansion of the operation.

The Dependency Curse

Contrary to what you might expect, the native tribes don't always win in the gambling competition—nor do the commercial giants like Genting, for that matter. The Seminole tribe, which operates seven casinos in Florida, beat Genting in that state. The Seminoles, Disney World and other business interests defeated a Genting proposal for a $3.8 billion casino resort in southern Florida, which they feared would cut back on their profits. The Mohegan Sun tribe in Connecticut also gambled and lost. The tribe had joined with a private developer and skipped across the border to New York to compete for one of the four casino sites in that state. Like Foxwoods in Connecticut the Mohegan tribe was suffering from a big debt brought on by an over-expansion of its existing casino. But the foray into New York didn't pay off. Genting was luckier this time. Relying again on the influence of big-time lobbying, campaign contributions and public-relations efforts, it won approval to build a $750 million casino resort, not near Manhattan, but in an economically distressed area to the north. While Genting couldn't buy its way into Florida, where Disney World reigns supreme, it did win the jackpot in New York in the area seeking gambling jobs.

Being a native tribe wasn't enough for the Mohegan Sun to prevail in New York. Five tribes in that state already have a monopoly for their casinos in other regions in exchange for a share of their revenue with the government, a trade-off the Shakopee Sioux have avoided in Minnesota, thereby assuring the millions for members there. Thus the Sioux enjoy their monopoly, while the New England market, including New York, is already saturated with casinos.

This account of the casino competition in New York is worth reciting in so much detail because it shows the intensity of the continuing battle among not only native tribes but also by a prosperous state for those gambling dollars. It also shows the power of competitors like Disney and Genting. And most of all it shows the reality that Indian tribes will no longer get an inside track to the casino riches, as they did at Mystic Lake in Minnesota, just because they are a victimized minority still owed on past debts.

And not just in New England. The gambling glut also forced a large commercial casino way down in Mississippi to shut down. What's more,

VII. Conclusion

MGM Resorts International, largest owner of casinos on the Los Vegas Strip, has reported a third-quarter loss, of all things, more evidence that the decline was no longer a threat, but a reality. Consider that casinos, both commercial and Indian, are now operating in almost 40 states. Even the Shakopee Sioux, co-featured in this account, reported a while back that their revenues had declined a bit, meaning they had less money to share with other tribes.

In Oregon the Klamaths, with their small casino, don't share the concern of many other tribes about a decline in the gambling industry, but like many tribes they worry not only about lack of jobs and economic development, but also about the dilution of their cultures as native people. Jobs and money are not everything. Many Klamaths have intermarried with people of other tribes or people of European descent. An obituary of Ian Michael Hoches Bettles noted that his Indian name was KinClane, meaning of "many nations." It was certainly appropriate for him, being of Aleut, Nez Perce, Cree. Klamath, Modoc, Wasco, Warm Springs and Navajo descent. Like many Klamaths, he died young at 33. (As we have observed, such a mix of cultures is not unusual among the Klamaths, any more than it is among Jewish people, as witness our three Jewish sons-in-law in our mixed family.)

Author David Treuer, himself a mix of Indian and Jewish blood, points out the difficulty of identifying who is "Indian" and who is not: "In all of us there is some Scottish blood, and Irish, too. Also French and German. And, going way back, African." In his book, "Rez Life," Treuer recounts how a black slave named Bonga, freed by his British owner around 1790, wound up in what became the Leech Lake reservation, married an Ojibway woman and there he stayed, as did his descendants, many of whom have the last name Bonga. How's that for a "native" name?

But does culture or identity matter that much, any more for natives than for the descendants of immigrants? Economist Tom Trulove, the longtime and astute student of the Klamath people, in a communication with this author, says it matters only to a point: "Like other groups their (Indian) ethnic heritage matters and is to be celebrated, but is separated from daily life and making a living. Getting to the point where kids go away to work and live and where there is a geographic place (center if you will) to which to return for celebrations, festivals, traditional observances is a very long process and, perhaps, not one that can be jump started."

So, in the long haul, will the Klamaths survive as an ethnic minority, while adapting to and accepting the demands of a middle-class America? Many have already and many more will. Klamath historian Alatorre, professing her pride in being a Klamath, answered in the affirmative when, as we have noted, she pointed out how her predecessors adjusted to naturally occurring global cooling and survived for thousands of years. What a great insight on adapting to climate changes long ago. Will the people of today be able to overcome the climate change brought about not just by the forces of nature but in large part by their own actions?

Young people will help answer the question, as they do in all populations facing profound change. Steve Lang may hint at the answer in his challenge to efforts by tribal elders to restore long-gone fish runs for people hardly expected to return to fish for sustainability. Some younger Klamaths also complain about leaders lacking in education, though some of them have performed quite ably. The emphasis on the need for education echoes the prescription of researcher Trulove, calling for an expansion of K-12 schooling to bring most Klamaths into the middle-class.

In the common cliché of journalism, time will tell, will tell what the future holds for Native Americans. For certain, the status quo will not prevail. As for now, the Klamaths are expanding, not retracting. Total tribal membership has risen from 2,100 when they lost federal status half a century ago, to more than 3,600 now under the federal umbrella. But those numbers partly reflect the desire of more natives to gain the jobs and benefits of this dependence on the government. Nationally, native population has doubled within a century.

As this writer has noted, conclusions about the outlook for natives are illusive. But one conclusion seems unassailable, that they are not going away. The Klamaths make that point: They have endured as a primitive people living off the land, to government wards on self-contained reservations, to 25 years on their own when their reservation and government

VII. Conclusion

benefits were terminated, to another quarter century back as wards of the government with a federally sanctioned tribal identity, but with half living in cities. Perhaps Native Americans generally survive partly because as a beleaguered, or a romanticized and patronized minority, they find strength in their cultures and identities (and they are many). Perhaps they also survive because, with dispersal beyond their reservations, they still get together in Barbara Alatorre's self-help organization in big-city Portland or employment centers in Minneapolis, developing a pan-Indian or generic identity transcending an individual tribal identity. Perhaps they reflect what happens to all tribal people when cast adrift, as this writer found in a journalistic assignment in South Africa, where tribal people go to the cities to cross religious and cultural bounds. Perhaps, perhaps, perhaps.

Meantime, Klamaths celebrate each year to mark their restoration as an official tribe, portrayed recently on the cover of their newspaper, tribal members wearing colorful attire, with feathered headdresses, problems forgotten, at least for now.

AFTERWORD

THE DEPENDENCY CURSE. That's the title I have given to this book. Is it descriptive, accurate, fair?

In looking for answers to that question, I have described the role of dependency in the lives of natives in two tribes, one in Oregon dependent on government and the other in Minnesota, on gambling. And in the beginning of this book, I noted that a native leader told me 50 years ago that a dependency on "free" money had impaired the will to work of his Klamath people, causing, in his opinion, the poverty of shabby homes and second-class status in a prosperous society. That changed: now the money is gone, and after a time of independence, the tribe depends on the benefits of government, but in many ways is no better off.

For a journalist with a personal and professional involvement in native life, that was disheartening. And just as disheartening are the examples of so many other native problems, indicating that so little has changed in the lives of so many of the first Americans. In a trip across the country, my wife and I found notable examples of this continuing tragedy. We drove by the Pine Ridge reservation in South Dakota, the home of the late Chief Red Cloud, whose tribe had once dominated one-fifth of the country; now reduced to debilitating poverty. From there we drove to the site of one of the natives' greatest victories, the annihilation of Lt. Col. George Armstrong Custer and

The Dependency Curse

more than 260 of his military men, who had been sent out to subdue them. Today, in the shadow of the hill of Custer's destruction in 1876, a cluster of Crow Indian homes is just as rundown as the dwellings lamented by Klamath leader Seldon Kirk, long ago.

You could call it ironic that some of the Crow had joined with Custer as scouts against rival tribes, especially the Sioux, a longstanding enemy. As far back as the early 1800s Sioux warriors raided one of the Crow villages and continued to push them aside in their relentless campaign to control a vast Upper Plains territory. The "romantics" who decry the government's takeover of native lands fail to mention that powerful Indian tribes like the Sioux and Comanches to the south were doing the same thing to expand their empires. So, the Crow and Apache—victims of the Comanches—allied with the American government to protect themselves from their rapacious rival tribes. It was a co-dependency (that word again), the government and the natives using each other for mutual benefit. I repeat my earlier point that the Klamaths sought and gained dependence on the government after a period of independence, thus showing the persistence of the dependency factor.

With Custer, the Crow natives were of course on the wrong side when the American officer and his troops fatally lost the battle of Little Bighorn, though they avoided his fate, leaving before the battle began. While losing that battle, however, Custer's people, the European occupiers, won the war and the territory once controlled by Red Cloud, whose Sioux warriors were among those who took on Custer's army. (Red Cloud had retired from the fight by then.) From the highway, meantime, my wife and I could see that many of the Crow remain in the shabby homes of poverty, as a dependent class, on a reservation that encompasses the battlefield. And what we saw is partly what is: The rates of poverty, unemployment and attempted suicide are way too high; educational attainment too low.

The Crow are seeking to reduce their dependence and their social pathology. But their timing is not good. They are expanding their small, isolated casino at a time of increasing competition for gambling dollars. And they are hoping to add to the development of their considerable coal

Afterword

resources at a time, similarly, of stiff competition from the country's burgeoning oil and natural gas production.)

Of course, in driving across the plains to Oregon, my wife and I didn't see much evidence of the marginal status of the natives in tourist literature related to Pine Ridge in South Dakota, the Crow in next-door Montana or the other, still-dependent native people. On the contrary, an attractive brochure produced by the South Dakota Department of Tourism touts the tribal lands, with a colorful cover of natives in traditional dress, replete with feathers. "Rich in history and culture, tribal lands offer something for visitors of all ages," says the brochure. Including casinos, powwows, native art markets, hunting and fishing and traditional foods along with "hospitality at its finest."

Some of the tribes also promote attractions on their reservations, such as cultural museums or a buffalo interpretive center of the Lower Brule Sioux tribe. The tribe doesn't mention that in earlier years white hunters killed tens of millions of the plains buffalo for the sale of their hides, depriving the natives of their livelihood and their independence. No longer could male members of the tribe hunt buffalo for food and other necessities; they were dependent on the government to satisfy their needs. No longer, moreover, would the male natives develop a sense of self-worth from hunting to meet those needs. As we have noted, native journalist Charles Trimble has attributed the social pathology of native people today to this lack of a useful role for male members of families.

Yes, education and jobs are crucial ingredients for most males in any cultural group to make it in the "real" world. Indeed, in our trip through native territory, we found a recognition of that truism in one of the tourist brochures. The Oglala Lakota Sioux tribe at Pine Ridge, that poster image of poverty, went beyond promoting tourist attractions to cite the Oglala Lakota College as evidence that education "is the key to overcoming poverty and its hideous effects on people." Another handout pointed to the Red Cloud Indian School as a fulfillment of Chief Red Cloud's dream in 1888 of building a school that would serve children on the Pine Ridge reservation.

The "hideous effects" were described so tellingly by Olowan Thunder

The Dependency Curse

Hawk Martinez in an interview with a writer for the National Geographic: An uncle had molested her when she was six and again when she was ten. "Afterward," she said, "he used words—he told me I was useless. I remember feeling such a deep pain that nothing and nobody could reach inside to take it away." She went on to say that once she was "looking down at the kitchen counter and seeing a knife. And suddenly that knife seemed like the only way to cut out every pain inside me. So I picked it up and started to saw though the skin on my wrist." But the irrepressible Martinez "snapped out of it," as she put it, and dropped the knife. The one-time drug-dealer is by now the mother of three and a self-appointed youth leader. In a culture she portrays as permeated with a sense of worthlessness, she has found self-worth. It's almost like our adopted native son, who was descending into severe alcoholism, and snapped out of it on his own, without drugs or therapy, to become a highly successful human being.

Oglala Sioux leaders are not alone in calling for education, from elementary to college level, to help overcome poverty and its debilitating effects on native people like Martinez. The need for education also was emphasized by some members of the Klamaths in Oregon, a focus of this book. In a sort of a putdown, one Klamath went so far as to complain about tribal leaders not being educated, as though that would account for the continuing problems in his tribe. The problem, as this author sees it, is that dependence has not produced the incentive to get an education and make it in the mainstream of life.

But dependence on the government can bring big benefits, really big ones, along with the negative byproducts. The U.S. Justice Department recently announced a settlement to pay $554 million to the Navaho nation for mismanaging its natural resources, including oil, coal and timber. Remember that the government made instant millionaires out of the Klamaths, in terms of today's dollar value, when it bought up and paid them for their land and timber. Nevertheless, for the Navahos, Klamaths and other tribes, lack of jobs is prompting a migration to the cities.

The cash cow of gambling also provides very big benefits for some tribes, but also carries a negative byproduct, as we have pointed out. Yes,

Afterword

dependency continues to be the underlying issue.

Dependency was not the issue I had intended to examine when, upon retirement after a long career in print journalism, I undertook this project on Native Americans. Going in, I planned to expose how the government had victimized the Klamath tribes of Oregon under a termination of their tribal status. See below on how that turned out. For background, I had learned about the tribes while working as a newspaper reporter one summer in a town near their Oregon reservation. Then, for the Oregon Journal in Portland, I had written that many Klamaths had indeed been victimized by nearby white merchants in their spending of money received from the government under the termination plan, as noted in this narrative. Now, with lots of time in retirement from my newspaper in Minneapolis, after 60 years of episodic reportage on native Americans, I would undertake a project on another example of "lo, the poor Indian," how the Klamaths had been screwed again, this time by the government itself in buying up their land under the termination plan. It fit the contours of the stereotype.

Sad to say for me in my pursuit of the tried and true story, it just wasn't true. Despite what their advocates and paid experts said, The Klamaths had not been cheated in the sale of their timber to the government; they had been paid a proper amount as determined in two independent evaluations; the second one demanded by the tribe, came in lower than the first. If they were victims of termination in other ways not yet publicly claimed, I couldn't find any examples of "other ways." So, winding up with a project in search of a story, I gave it up. Well, I gave up that version of the "story," but as I wrote in the introduction of this book, I didn't give up on finding another story on the travail of the native population. I didn't give up because family and professional involvements made the subject of great interest to me. And thus was born this book, on dependency as a possible major cause of the long-standing social problems of the Klamaths and other Native Americans. Along the way of my research, I learned a lot to challenge my conventional thinking on "lo, the poor Indian." I learned about the realistic views of at least one native leader, the questionable assertions of others, the simplistic and inaccurate rendering of Indian history, and, as could be expected, the

The Dependency Curse

mixed reactions to the dependency issue I had posited. Quite a learning experience.

Consider Lynn Schonchin, a tribal elder approaching age 70, great grandson of Modoc freedom fighter Schonchin John, raised by his grandparents, victim of lawyers, accountants and even his father for taking most of his termination money, fire-fighter for the Forest Service, three times elected chairman of the Klamaths, high school teacher and counselor as well as general manager of the tribal nation, insistent he be fired as manager when caught gambling with tribal funds in the Klamath casino, self-professed idiot for leaving his wife of 42 years who was trying to help him during this personal disaster. And speaker of unpleasant truth about prospects for the Klamaths.

I have recounted much of Schonchin's personal and professional life in this narrative, gathered in four interviews, because it is so reflective of the Klamath situation. Personal integrity and straight talk are paramount in that life. When tribal leaders offered him a suspension for his gambling misconduct, he insisted on being fired as manager as just due for what he did, then repaying the money and working for the tribe in lesser jobs. And when some Klamath leaders follow the popular political path in calling for the return of their forested land (for which the tribe has been paid), he says it doesn't have much of a chance. And when a Modoc splinter group, from his tribe, seeks to split off into a separate nation. he said, in an elaboration of an assessment I made earlier, "It's a joke…They can't even get along with their own people. One of the guys is my cousin. The motive is money. They think if they have a new tribe they can get land. All it does is cause more division. It doesn't help matters. This is the fifth or sixth time it has come up. It is not going anywhere. The guy leading it is not even an Indian. He's got a pipe dream."

Remember that the Modocs, sometimes enemies of the Klamaths in earlier years, chafed under the domineering Klamaths when forced by the government to leave their homeland and live with them on the Klamath reservation. Ultimately they went to war to reclaim their homeland and their freedom. As we should know, much of history is determined by those who

Afterword

describe it, and Schonchin the history teacher has his version of that war, a war on the Modocs, not the Modoc war, he says. When it was over, the government executed 38 Modocs, including Schonchin's great grandfather, Schonchin John. Why the unprecedented executions? Partly because a Modoc leader killed an army general (Canby), the first general killed in war up to then. Then there was the humiliation and embarrassment over a few dozen Modocs holding off the superior forces of the army for months. (Schonchin John's son, Peter, one of the fighters, was sent to Oklahoma as a "prisoner of war.") And don't forget the false allegation, as descendent Lynn Schonchin sees it, that the Modocs had massacred a bunch of white settlers.

But descendants of those oppressed people, like Lynn Schonchin, don't waste time lamenting the past. Schonchin has played a major role in the leadership of the combined two tribes (along with the Yahooskin band), and now reflects on the here and now, like the recent recall of tribal leaders. The problem, he says is that they "were not getting things done. People were unhappy wth the way things were going. There were no particulars, and the leadership was not totally responsible. Benefits were being cut; services were being cut (because federal funding was reduced)." I will add that the new chairman in the recall has since been replaced by another chairman, each with a different prescription to treat the Klamath problems. (I am reminded that the daughter of a Klamath elder once told me that each new leader puts forth a new plan, rather than build on what has been done already, thus bringing about no real change.)

Schonchin lays out the naked truth about the present Klamath situation: that there are few jobs on the reservation and poor prospects for economic development, a dismal outlook. Beyond that, half or more of the government and tribal jobs are filled by outsiders because tribal members lack experience for the work. And they lack experience because outside employers have been reluctant to hire "Indians." "Go down Main Street," Schonchin says, "and you will see one Indian, and one at Walmart. The attitude is that you Indians are getting all this government money, free health care and all that, so we don't need to hire you." The result, he says, is lots of unemployment and dependency (there's that word again). Meantime, he

The Dependency Curse

continues, "our tribal government and economic development people have pie in the sky. They won't do it (a project) unless it makes a million, they should acquire some small businesses and put people to work." That is what I mean by straight talk, about both his people and the "others."

And realistic talk. Schonchin doesn't portray Klamaths as the only victims of the piece. As he sees it, the people of Klamath County, Indian and non-Indian, have suffered from a decline of the forest-based economy, shown by the demise of 20 lumber mills in recent decades. It's been boom or bust (now more bust) for the richest and the poorest, he says; you see newly empty stores weekly, especially those locally owned. Prospects for growth? Not good. Development of a biomass industry, exploiting wood waste? "It will never happen," he says. Jobs in agriculture? A drop in the bucket, hiring mostly migrant labor," he adds. "Pie in the sky" development proposals that don't make it? I will answer that, pointing to the continued touting of questionable plans for the so-called Mazama tract in the northern reaches of the former reservation, and to expansion of the Klamath casino, a failed plan that cost the tribe $2 million. (The small casino provided a token $1,000 per tribal member in a recent year; compare that to the million per year for members of the Shakopee Sioux tribe In Minnesota.)

Schonchin agrees with icon Seldon Kirk on the deleterious effects of dependency, which the government created, he claims, when it established the reservation system. It should be noted that the government did make fumbling efforts to move Klamaths from dependence to independence, efforts that failed partly because the natives apparently preferred a certain amount of dependence. (So what else is new? Corporations, farmers and homeowners don't want to give up the subsidies and tax breaks that make them partly dependent on the government many criticize as too big.)

Actually, for all the problems associated with dependency, the Klamaths have maintained their membership through times of dependence and independence in the 150 years since they were forced onto a reservation, indicating the strength of their cultural and genetic ties. But it may be more than that, it may be, as I have said, that dependency itself is an addictive attraction. Consider that their membership shot up by almost two-thirds in the

Afterword

past quarter of a century, from 2,086 to 3,600, when, after a lengthy stretch of independence, the government restored their tribal status and their dependence, making them eligible for the full benefits of being wards of the government. They wanted it.

For the future, however, Schonchin puts his faith not in a dependency status but in a tribal status, in the tribe taking care of its members, and a new attitude of members about the importance of the tribe. "They are in their 30s," he says of these members. "I have a lot of faith in them. Those who came after termination; watch them. They say, this is who we are. They visit me and other older Indians. They ask about our culture and history. They are not just the college graduates; they are everybody. I am their teacher."

Still, Schonchin is not so naïve as to believe that identity and tribalism will solve the problems of natives in Oregon and beyond. As I have reported in this narrative, other Klamaths agree with him that they must get educations, go where the jobs are, be independent, make periodic visits to their homeland, all the while maintaining their culture and identity. Many are doing just that; some are young, others are of middle age and beyond. (Of course, tribalism cuts two ways, provides support for many ethnic, religious or national peoples, yet, when taken to extremes, has led to horrific conflict in the Middle East and Africa.)

To maintain awareness of their culture, the Klamath tribes sponsor camps each summer to teach children about the language, history and traditional practices of their ancestors, For them, it's more than talk; they visit cultural and plant-gathering sites, even build duck decoys on Upper Klamath Lake.

Gordon Bettles has done his part to preserve the culture and help the people of the Klamath tribes. He rose from the poverty of seven living in two rooms, no running water, no bathroom. He rose from that to get university degrees, work with at-risk youths and then for many years serve as cultural director. He has also assumed the role of protector of the image of the Klamaths. When I sent him a copy of an article that I turned into this book, he wrote back, "I don't like the prominence you gave regarding my family. It casts an unfair pall over the tribe as you have made a comparison of

Klamath Indian families." Accordingly, he asked that I remove him and his family from the story. (Another native scholar asked the same; more on him later.) That was the last I heard from him, after he had generously consented to an interview.

Bettles knows today the extremes of family life among the Klamaths, he being among the educated elite. But he doesn't exploit his status, preferring, like Schonchin, to emphasize the enduring culture of his tribe. For many years maintaining that culture of the Native American way was an "uphill battle," according to a newspaper profile of Bettles, titled "keepers of the flame." It was an "uphill battle" when, under termination, the government took away the tribal status of the Klamaths. Bettles told author Ulrich that termination became personal for him when in college some drunk Indian students "beat me up, called me a sell-out" for giving up tribal recognition in exchange for money. "I had black eyes for three weeks," he said. "I couldn't leave my room for two days. Indian girls brought food finally."

Now, with the Klamaths officially restored as a tribe for almost three decades, Bettles still talks of reclaiming a tribal unity that had been sundered during termination. Asked about the continuing dependency on government, he suggests, among other things, the creation of jobs at the likes of a truck stop and motel, recreational and tourist attractions, along with other businesses in different areas, not just at or near the reservation. But the key question remains, why is it taking so long to develop these enterprises to help make the tribe self-supporting? "Bettles answers: "When you drop an economic bomb on a group of people, either they scatter or hunker down and hide, or do something about it. They all did some of that…The tribe has to come back together as a solid tribe to make things happen."

No, the tribe has not been solid, certainly not in the violence of the recall battle, that three times led to the calling of sheriff's deputies to restore the peace. Gary Frost called for unity after being elected chairman as a result of the attempted recall, led by his wife. Don Gentry, who replaced Frost in the next election, took a new tack in seeking to represent the diversity of views. Had he given up on achieving unity? Bettles knows about all this.

With the passage of so much time and so little accomplished, all the talk of making things happen could be called wishful thinking, especially considering the limited potential of the proposals for economic development without a land base. Like Schonchin, however, Bettles sees hope in a new generation of Klamaths, learning to exist as Indian people in the general community, going forward, not backward to be fenced in a reservation any more. Bettles lives in Eugene to the north, and speaks for the majority of Klamaths who also live away. Again, like Schonchin, he sees in the eyes of the new generation, "a brightness that in my generation was dimmed" (presumably, he means dimmed by termination).

Klamath scholar Tom Ball, another descendent of a Modoc freedom fighter, simply rejects any concern about dependency on government. The Klamaths, he says, "are not a dependent sovereign. We are a sovereign period. We signed treaties as a sovereign nation and we are." I asked, is this an identity issue? "That's part of it," he answered. "But for me the word sovereignty implies that no one else can tell you or define who you are. And we have let them treat us as a domestic sovereign. Identity is huge and huge for our children."

In short, as Ball sees it, the Modocs lost their war against the government, but remain entitled to government support under the earlier treaty that forced them to live with the Klamaths. Ball speaks with considerable Indian credibility, being both a Klamath and great grandson of Captain Jack, who led the Modocs in that war and was executed for killing the army general. Like Schonchin, also part Modoc, he has been deeply involved in Klamath affairs, doing extensive research on the tribes for his doctoral degree and also serving briefly as chairman before moving ultimately to Eugene to become an assistant vice-president at the University of Oregon.

Rather than blame dependency for the ills of Native Americans, he has concluded that the Klamaths suffer from a continuing trauma, like soldiers in a war. He explained, "I went to a workshop on post-traumatic stress disorder. They talked mainly about Vietnam veterans. My jaw just about dropped open and my eyes popped out, because as they went through all those symptoms, all the things these Vietnam veterans were experiencing, it looked and sounded just like what our tribal members were going through.

The Dependency Curse

This led me to believe that trauma from the experience of termination was devastating our people. It was the only thing that was different between us and other Indians." As I have noted, his research for his doctorate supported that thesis, in an admittedly limited way.

Ball attributes lack of progress on economic development to the tribe's remote location and loss of its land base in termination. But he says the building of a casino is a source of pride, showing "we can build something and manage it." This pride may partly explain why he helped me so much in my research, setting up meetings with librarians and listing source material when I came to Eugene to see him. On the other hand, Ball wanted me to get approval of tribal government before submitting my work for publication. The tribe, he said, is not open to the public because openness has been turned against them. I might say it is a defensiveness, based on the fear of being put in a bad light, that is common in beleaguered minority groups. In my case, Ball told a tribal official that my article most likely would be favorable to the Klamaths, but in view of the ongoing issue of water rights "we need to be ever vigilant on what is printed about us."

In reviewing Tom Ball's life story for this book, I am struck by the depth of his involvement with the Klamaths, even though he was born in big-city Portland, not the reservation (his father moved there to work in the shipyards in World War II). That involvement is not surprising, however, considering that he is the nephew of the venerated Klamath chairman Seldon Kirk, as well as being related to the rebel Modoc leader Captain Jack. Those leadership genetics, along with his identification with Klamath culture, obviously had much to do with his attraction to the tribe, regardless of where he lived. As a Portland resident, he also got acquainted with Klamaths by spending summers with an uncle at the reservation and by taking part in Barbara Alatorre's intertribal organization of Portland Indians. Remember he talked of urban natives periodically visiting the reservation. You might call it a cultural and relational inter-dependency (or the native tribalism cited by Schonchin).

While Ball rejects dependency as a cause of the Klamath problems, he apparently suffered earlier from a dependency of his own, on alcohol.

Afterword

Ironically, in his research findings he had attributed the Klamath's social pathologies, including pervasive alcoholism, to the termination trauma of losing tribal status. In his interview with author Roberta Ulrich, he talked of leaving a teaching job "because he fell off the wagon and thought kids deserved better." A gambling dependency led to Schonchin's loss of his tribal management position. Dependency, dependency. It runs through this narrative on the plight of Native Americans.

As you know, I first came across the dependency issue many years ago in an interview with Klamath leader Seldon Kirk. Then I found a powerful presentation on the issue by Minnesota Appellate Judge James Randall, a long-time advocate, benefactor and friend of Native Americans. I have mentioned how he tore into beer companies for aiding and abetting alcoholism on the Pine Ridge reservation. Earlier he cited how government/ward status continued "to keep Indian people on reservations in a tribal state of dependency on either state and federal handouts or expansion of the increasingly unaccountable gambling." (The tiny Mdewakanton Sioux tribe in Minnesota has been able to depend entirely on gambling by maintaining a casino monopoly in its area through effective lobbying of state government and dispersal of generous funds to other tribes. The Sioux tribe also opened up its rolls to more members, thus sharing the profits more widely and avoiding complaints from natives who would otherwise be outsiders. (More on that later.) On the other hand, some eastern tribes must compete with commercial, non-Indian casinos, who themselves are suffering from a decline in the gambling mania.

A decline in commercial gambling? Is that possible? Yes. As I mentioned earlier several casinos in Atlantic City, an epicenter of a wagering culture, have shut down, throwing thousands of people out of work. But that has not deterred New York voters from approving seven casinos in that state, for jobs and tax revenue of course. Indian casinos competing with each other? We do know that, but they aren't the only ones worried about competition. Consider the situation in New York, where upstate casino proponents were worried sick about plans—since deterred—for a giant casino complex near New York City, which they feared would attract an international clientele and deprive them of a plethora of patrons. Beyond that, New York is part of the northeast region, which is nearly saturated with 51 casinos.

In a sense, states like New York want to build a certain dependence on gambling, just as some native tribes have done, maybe to their long-range detriment. As I have noted in this narrative, some prominent native leaders and advocates have expressed concern about the gambling dependency for natives. One of the most forceful proponents of this view is Minnesota jurist Randall in opposing the allegedly deleterious "state of dependency" on casinos, as well as on government, under questionable claims of independent sovereignty to justify their dependence. I should point out that of all non-natives, Randall has a great deal of cachet to express these concerns. The judge, now retired, hardly qualifies as a bleeding-heart liberal with a romantic view of Native Americans. He talks straight. As related by the late native journalist Bill Lawrence, he was involved with natives for decades, representing native people for many years while practicing law in northern Minnesota, helping build a school for native children in Alaska, promoting fishing and gathering rights of natives in Canada, supporting educational opportunities for native high-school students, working with native prison inmates, maintaining friendships with many natives. And writing persuasive legal briefs in court cases on their behalf, as he sees it. The list goes on.

As I have emphasized, some native leaders also express concern about this dependency. When I showed an excerpt of my narrative on this dependency to native journalist Charles Trimble, he responded, "right on the money." I cite his reaction not as an ironclad defense of my thesis, which is certainly not universally accepted, but as an indication that it is viewed as highly credible from deep in the native community. Trimble was born and raised in the Pine Ridge Indian reservation among a Oglala Sioux population ravaged by alcoholism and other social plagues. "In tribal societies on the plains," he has said, "the father had a central role in the family as provider." Now government or gambling is often the provider, and many men have no useful role. Result? Alienation, drinking and drugs. We well know that sad story, and not just at Pine Ridge.

Veteran native journalist Tim Giago also responded favorably to what I

Afterword

had written, and suggested that I seek publication as a series in Native Sun News, a suggestion I deferred in favor first of gaining wider dissemination of my provocative thesis, claiming dependency as a major cause of the seemingly intractable problems of Native Americans. Giago, a founder of four Indian publications and an award-winning columnist, has warned of new social problems arising from a gambling addiction among native people ensconced at the gaming tables and slot machines of their own casinos. As I have noted, Lynn Schonchin of the Klamaths was one of them.

I have raised the open question of how long the gambling boom, especially among native tribes, will last. Maybe not so long, as shown in the closing of those commercial casinos in iconic gambling den Atlantic City. Economist David Bunting, who has studied the Klamaths, put forth some historical perspective in an email to me. As he points out, various ethnic groups have used their "native" affiliations for economic gains. Indians are using theirs for exclusive casino rights. How long that will last, he says, is anyone's guess. But in the Pacific Northwest many native groups are trying to climb aboard the casino money train. "As competition develops," he says, "some will fail." Beyond that, Bunting doesn't think that special legal status that has economic consequences—insert here treat rights in perpetuity—has long run viability. The Klamaths learned that when the government bought up and paid for their timber resources, making them independent regardless of any treaty obligations.

For more historical perspective, Bunting's colleague, economist Tom Trulove, observes that back to ancient times native people depended for survival on the tribe (not government, I would add), but this dependence is in some ways a weakness in today's world. He goes on, "Perhaps it is not the drink, drugs, mixing of ancient tribes, but rather the great difficulty in overcoming the 'wisdom' of centuries so that like other ethnic groups, their ethnic heritage matters and is to be celebrated but is separate from daily life and making a living."

And that is exactly what is happening. In a great migration, similar to the movement of African Americans from south to north, some two-thirds of natives have left their reservation, many to make a living in the real world

(Klamaths are slower to move; half having gone elsewhere). You look around the world and you see the same movement from the countryside to jobs in the cities, creating in some cases an unmanageable metropolis like Mexico City. (I know, I've been there.)

As I have noted, some Klamaths, like natural resources director Elwood Miller, plan to stay at the reservation but he is not happy about what has been done to exercise treaty rights since tribal status was restored. The tribe, he told author Ulrich, should pick up the pace on planning and move beyond planning to create job-producing enterprises, such as a truck stop that would employ 20 people, along with a motel and bingo operation to supplement the casino. So far, job creation has been too little and late, and doomed to remain so in view of the lack of the forest resource that had supported the tribe.

But working and making a living has not been a problem for Klamaths like Theodore Crume, now in his 80s, who worked as a farmer, rancher and truck driver. He has a simple desire for native people: "We don't want to be white people. We just want to be people. Want to make a living." Now that is a realistic desire, because being white doesn't mean much, considering all the ethnic and national groups among them, any more than being "Indian" means much considering there are more than 500 tribes of differing cultures, from one-time hunters of buffalo on the Great Plains to fishermen in the Pacific Northwest.

These distinctions don't mean much either in our large, mixed family of many ethnic and national backgrounds, which I described early in this book. As "white" liberals, we parents can count adult children and grandchildren of conservative to liberal leanings, of varying degrees of work ethic from strong to episodic, and of extremes in conformance or non-conformance to societal norms, from criminal to total patriotic adherence. And I can't forget the tragedy of the early death of a Native-American daughter, who, like so many natives, died way too early. That's one reason why in this book I have tried to portray a mixed account of the possible causes of the continued social pathology of Native Americans, about whom I know quite a bit from personal and journalistic experience. But, as I have written, my

Afterword

emphasis on this "pathology" is far from being universally accepted by native people. I am not surprised about that, having been challenged many times by people I have accused of wrongdoing in more than two decades of investigative reporting for my newspaper. But I was taken aback, severely so, about the ultimate reaction of a long-time friend, Gerald Vizenor, himself a native of considerable credibility as professor at a prestigious university, champion of native causes, social activist, prison counselor, newspaper journalist, author of more than two dozen books, many on native culture and, most telling, critic of marauding members of the American Indian Movement, which he had helped to found. For that he received threats to his life, which he laughed about. This is not to mention his being a poet and a plumber, having replaced the kitchen plumbing in our old house. Such was our long and enduring friendship that my wife dubbed him as our eighth adopted family member.

Thus I was not surprised when he challenged my portrayal of natives as victims rather than survivors, himself the survivor (or victim?) of a tumultuous childhood: his father murdered at age 26, his mother who had too many problems of her own to contend with a contentious son, but foster parents who did well by him. For all of that, or because of it, he went on to be a success in so many ways. (In our family, he most identifies with our native son, the highly successful firefighter, carpenter, mechanic, husband and father of three.) But I was surprised at how he reacted to my email message referring to the "pathology" of native people. The tone and language of his response was very bothersome, as in "Joe, your use of the word 'pathology' is not acceptable in any sense of a discussion about Native Americans. I strongly protest your use of the word in the context of your essay. You seem determined to contribute to the victimry of Native Americans." Wow, I was so upset about this unfriendly message that I was prompted to respond in kind: "Your comments are duly noted." And that led him to tell me, "I have decided not to allow you to quote me in your essay. So, please remove any reference to me and quotations attributed to me." This came after he accepted without objection what I planned to say about his views in my essay, and after he told me how to identify his university status, and after

The Dependency Curse

I had agreed with some of his critiques of what I was writing. By the way, my use of the word "pathology," as applied to the situation of many natives today, is arguable, but defensible.

As noted above, I chose the totally defensible term, "social pathology," as propounded by scholar Yellow Horse Brave Heart. But she also referred to drinking behavior among natives as usually "pathological," using one word as I had done in my message to scholar Vizenor. She pointed out that their alcohol death rate has been more than five times the national average, exerting a "devastating effect on the health and morale of Indian people." Pathology, according to the Webster dictionary, is related to disease, and alcoholism is certainly that. (All natives, or all everybody, including Yellow Horse, Vizenor and myself, are supposed to think alike? Hardly.)

What bothered me most about Vizenor's reaction was that this was coming from the ultimate contrarian, who took on many of the romantic stereotypes of Native Americans, Indians having a special way with children, exercising a profound reverence for the earth and acting as protectors of the environment? His take on these appellations is worth quoting in full: "Like the Caucasian invaders, some of the original inhabitants measured up to the romantic ideals, although some of their 'ideals' were merely creations of the late-coming settlers. Others ignored or defied the ideals, out of circumstance or inclination. In early years, many denuded the land where they lived, and moved on. In later years, others suffered from the dysfunctional family life of poverty. How could anyone expect them to be different?" (I will add that many of the "original inhabitants" of America themselves, including the Klamaths, are descendants of "invaders" or migrants from Asia thousands of years ago, when they crossed over the land mass that is now the Bering Sea.)

Of course, you can't take back quotes freely given. My response to his demand that I do so was "Jerry, your last two messages make me sad. I thought we were friends. What happened?" In the more than two years after sending that message, I had not heard from Vizenor.

In spite of this regrettable interchange, I will let Vizenor have the last word, which he had put forth earlier in an email to me: "Family and

Afterword

individual poverty and generations of dependency can be found everywhere in the world. So, what is unique about your point of native dependency on reservations? Once again you must provide some historical background and discuss federal policy." (Which I have tried to do.)

Well, not exactly the last word. I do owe it to you readers to speculate on why Vizenor cut me off after our long friendship. I think the answer may relate to identity, his identity as a native American and a reluctance to accept that identity to be tarnished, in this case as a victimized people dependent on government or gambling. Others have said much the same. Gordon Bettles, as a highly successful native, as is Vizenor, expressed concern about my touting his success to the detriment of less-successful Klamaths. Tom Ball just plain rejected the concept of dependent sovereign, saying his people are sovereign, period. He was not born on the reservation, but got a sense of identity partly from his association with Barbara Alatorre's small organization of natives, including Klamaths, almost a reservation itself in big-city Portland. She fiercely maintains her identity as a Klamath, serves as their historian and becomes upset when tribal officials don't measure up to her standards. Lynn Schonchin, the history teacher, counselor on culture for his grandchildren and the state police, descendent of a tribal freedom fighter, said he felt as if his identity had been stripped away when the government terminated tribal status for the Klamaths. The tribe got back its identify, even if at the expense of becoming dependent on the government. It's a tribal identity, much as the Irish maintain their self-worth as Irish, he said.

As you readers well know by now, the theme of this book deals with the dependency problem of Native Americans, and identity is part of the issue. I contend that an over- dependency on identity restricts the freedom of individuals to reach out to the broader world of ideas and careers—and thus jobs. In any event, the individual must decide whether identity is important. As I have noted, in our large family of differing racial identities, not one family member has considered it all that important, an exception being a grandchild. As one son describes himself, he is an American. As for me, I never really professed any identification with my German, Swiss and Dutch heritage. My spouse is just as removed from her Swedish heritage. From a broader perspective, a rigid adherence to tribal and religious identify has led to horrendous conflict within and between societies. (In this country, Tea Party rigidity, as a dominant influence in the Republican party, contributes greatly to the dysfunction of the U.S. Congress today.)

Clarence Page, the exceedingly astute African-American columnist for the Chicago Tribune, argues that political parties and voters must reach across these tribal lines to avoid doom in our information age of rigid and fragmented media, from TV talk shows, to social networks to targeted advertising markets. Amen. Native Americans are headed in that direction, with a majority now living away from reservation "ghettos," mostly in urban areas. They aren't necessarily giving up their tribal identity, but that is not the driving force of their lives. For many of them, their overall future as successful Americans, rather than dependent Americans, is yet to be determined.

As I close this book, I will reiterate what I have earlier discussed, that is, why I have given so much attention to a small remote native tribe in southern Oregon. I have done so because the Klamaths have been through every phase of tribal and government involvement, and not only survived, but thrived. In many ways they represent the experience of most of the original Americans. Early on they subsisted on the "fruit" of their land, living a hard life, independently but primitively. Then came the government, making them dependent on that government for food and material supplies on a reservation. The reason: To stop them from attacking white settlers and, as the government saw it, to protect them from the sometimes violent settlers. In a typical reaction to that forced settlement, a segment of the Klamaths, the Modoc tribe, fought the army valiantly, without success, to regain its homeland. They had been displaced, while the original Klamaths kept much of their homeland, located within the reservation.

As I have observed, the Klamaths enjoyed a semi-independence in the early 1900s when they began receiving payments from sales of their timber resource, but they were dependent on that free money without having to work for it, or develop the self-worth essential to human wellbeing. During this extended time the government first tried, through ill-conceived plans,

Afterword

to "make" the natives independent, following which Washington nationally gave natives the opportunity to individually own tracts of reservation land, which many Klamaths and others leased or sold to whites to their long-range detriment. The story goes on, to the ultimate experiment in creating native independence, the government buying the reservation and its extremely valuable forest resource for huge payments to the natives, almost like lottery or inheritance money. At long last, the Klamaths, and some other tribes, were independent, free of government domination and benefits. Nirvana? Hardly. Like many people who suddenly receive large fortunes, many spent much of it and sought the return of government sanctioned tribal status, dependent on that government. And that is where they are today. And so goes the story of the Klamaths and much of native America, to be continued.

Along the way in telling this story, I have dealt head-on with some of the stereotypes of the "Indian problem," such as the common critique of the government for taking over most of the native land. True, the government and its army did it. But they were not the first. In fact, two powerful tribes, the Sioux and Comanches, fought rival tribes to take over huge parts of America in the 1800s, creating empires in the colonial way, and in turn lost most of it to the more powerful, invading Europeans. No doubt, the Europeans were brutal in their wars to supplant the natives, but the natives were just as brutal, if not more so, in their fight to gain and maintain their territory and to wreak vengeance for what had happened to them: the white traders ripping them off and plying them with alcohol, the government failing to live up to its promises, and much, much more. So they resorted at times to the beheadings, mutilation and massacres we still see today in "tribal" conflicts of the non-native variety. (I won't go into the conflicts, even violence sometimes, though seldom, within most families, including a large one such as ours of native and other ethnic backgrounds.) And slavery? While the U.S. government tolerated the enslavement of millions of Africans, the Klamaths took a small number by comparison to trade for horses, a much sought commodity. And a United Nations report cited slavery and the trafficking of children even today.

The Dependency Curse

Let's not forget, moreover, the stereotype of the noble Indians united in the fight against the army to retain or regain their territories. As we have seen in this review of history, many Indians sided with the white army or remained neutral. Some served as scouts for the army in battles against rival tribes, and others had adapted to their new situation and opposed going to war, even warning whites of the threat of hostile Indians, or forming the equivalent of peace parties.

One important stereotype that has been shattered more than once is the belief that the first Americans have treaty rights with the government in perpetuity. What the government giveth, even through treaties, the government can taketh away, as it did in buying the Klamath resources and stripping the natives of tribal status. In a lesser way, the federal government temporarily took away the right of the Mdewakanton Sioux to decide on membership when it overruled a vote by the tribe to waive blood requirements, so as to share casino wealth with descendants of current and former tribal members. Conflict of interest questions had been raised about the eligibility of some Sioux voters who stood to benefit financially from the dropping of the blood requirement. Ironically, that federal decision was made by Ada Deer, a native champion of treaty rights then serving as director of the Bureau of Indian Affairs. Ultimately the tribe voted to reaffirm the so-called blood quantum standard, while "adopting" additional members to sidestep the requirement. It took more than a decade for a federal court to deal with a series of actions and finally settle that dispute, citing native treaty rights to decide on membership. It was among many of the tribal battles across the nation over who gets casino profits, reflecting the dependency thereon.

On the other hand, one enduring "stereotype," if you want to call it that, can be applied to everyone, native or not and helps to explain their diversity. The fact is that we are all subject to the good and the bad of human nature, despite the romantic view of the "goodness" of the first Americans. Generally, though in fits and starts, the human condition improves as time goes on. The history of the Klamaths and other tribes shows conclusively that they are no more "good" than anyone else. For sure, however, the

Afterword

Klamaths—the feature of this book—have come a long way from their primitive lives in years past, and now are dealing with the good and bad of dependence on government or gambling. As are most other natives (and so many whites). Whew, enough of that speech.

Over the long, long haul, the question for all Native Americans, as I see it, is whether they will maintain that dependence based on a reservations system forced on them long ago or merge into the main society, as many are now doing, while maintaining their identity, as many other people do. I return to Judge Randall for a final thought: "We have the power and the right to end the present system of red apartheid in this country, of wardship and of dependency, all cloaked in the myth of sovereignty. But, do we have the will?" I would add, it's not so much what "we" can or should do, but what the original Americans, along with the government, want to do, and are doing.

And what they are doing goes far beyond enduring a "red apartheid" or the negatives of dependency. They are resolutely maintaining their status as Indians, as descendants of the original Americans, as a distinct racial and ethnic group, as a people with a common bonding. That's true of the Klamaths and the Mdewakanton Sioux, whether they live on a reservation, a small town or the city. It's even true, to make the point a compelling one, of the Lumbee Indians of North Carolina, who are not recognized by the federal government as a tribe and have no reservation on which to live, yet are close to being economically self-sufficient while being racially deterministic.

And the greatly diminished number of natives who live on reservations continue to reap the benefits of their dependence on government, whether in free health care—a great benefit—or in subsidies for their governments and social programs. Federal courts, enforcing their long-standing treaty rights, are their best champions, as in the awarding of $554 million to the Navahos for government mismanagement of their natural resources.

You may hear the "romantic talk" of the noble natives from some whites, but not from people in the Klamath, Sioux and Lumbee people, or from Cherokee educator Marvin Buzzard. "We've been sold the notion, not

The Dependency Curse

just by the larger society, but by ourselves, that Indians are noncompetitive, that they don't care about money, that if they don't own anything, that is an expression of their 'Indianness.' This sort of thing is both racist and romantic, and it abets a lot of the self-destructive behavior that is out there." He went on to say that any notion that natives should live in isolation from contact with whites is absurd. "The most important thing education can do is give kids a choice about how to live their lives. Think of it as providing the weapons of survival for the modern warrior." That's good stuff.

But not as good as the final quest for survival by Chief Red Cloud of the Sioux. He adapted to a new reality when, after ruthlessly pushing aside other tribes to dominate a big part of America, from Minnesota to the Rockies, he was pushed aside himself by historical forces, as one writer put it. He knew he had to adapt to that new reality and he did, agreeing to peace with his "enemy." And on a personal level, seeking good schools for his children, and better land than what was given to his Sioux nation at Pine Ridge. He was honored in his death, but as a "modern warrior" he was not able to to get much of a better lot for the survival of his people at that reservation, lacking the timber of the Klamaths or the mineral resources of the Navaho to the south.

Navaho? We were there. On our way home from the West Coast on Interstate 40, my wife and I came across the sign, "Entering Navaho Nation." Indeed, covering parts of New Mexico, Arizona and Utah, this nation is the home of the second largest American tribe of almost 270,000 people, on the largest reservation in the country, larger than Ireland. Again, we encountered the dependency problem of native Americans. Well into the 20th century the Navaho relied mostly on farming and livestock to support themselves. But poorly applied government policies to reduce their herds and prevent overgrazing gradually took away much of their livelihood and made them a dependent people, dependent, like the Klamaths, partly on the government. Today many of the Navaho, even with their coal resources, are not so prosperous. We read about how so many of them lack clean water, drove by okay housing as well as tiny rundown homes and small trailers, amid dead cars and clutter, past the "hot slots" casinos, small and large,

Afterword

offering help but no final solution to the problems in Native America, past the stunning painted rock formations and the desolate nothingness of the desert, past the billboards touting native products of rugs and jewelry, some authenticated and some not, stopped at a MacDonalds where four natives were manipulating their smart phones. And then we learned that the Navaho are seriously considering whether to allow same-sex marriage among tribal members. That is a bit unusual, for a tradition-bound tribe like the Navaho. Or is it?

We continued along the freeway to Texas, once part of a vast empire that the powerful Comanche tribe had built through the brutal conquest of rival tribes, but not the conquest of the long-time enemy Navaho, despite many clashes. (The Comanche are not so powerful now, having been reduced from 45,000 members to less than half that, living mostly in Oklahoma, without a reservation.) Like the earlier trip West through the Dakotas, this return offered depressing vignettes of poverty and second-class status, all documented for the Navaho and so many other native tribes. Oh yes, the Navaho have four casinos, along with income from coal mining and a tourist trade, and are pushing more economic development to overcome their dependence on government. But the people still suffer from high unemployment, a high dropout rate in their schools and a high poverty level, some of them living in remote homes without telephone, plumbing or public utility services. Not to mention a severe drinking and drunk driving problem.

Big-time problems? Yes, but inspiring responses. Veteran Navaho lawmaker Edmund Yazzie is trying to make things better for his people. He's a leader of a heavy metal band (that's right, heavy metal in Navaho land) that pushes positive tunes to young people disillusioned over reservation troubles, tunes like "Move on" and "Live For Something, Die for Nothing." The band was formed out of reaction to a rash of suicides of young native people, 15 taking their lives in just two years. Two were friends of Yazzie's son Darius, 22, frontman for the band. I came across the "Rez Metal" story in the New York Times, which does such a good job of reporting on the ups and downs of the original Americans.

The Dependency Curse

Yazzie's band resonates with natives beyond the young. A pastor, Tim Castillo, 46, asked at a recent performance if the band would play at his church, figuring parishioners would relate to it's aggressive sound and benefit from its you-can-do-it ethos. He explained, "Our church is filled with people coming out of addiction, coming out of prison, broken homes, poverty, abuse. There's not a lot of positive."

I was not surprised to learn about the plight of the Navaho, or of an upbeat response, as I concluded my research and writing about the curse of dependency on Native Americans. I well remember Klamath scholar Tom Ball pointing out that the original Americans are still here after all these centuries, and will be for centuries to come.

Yes, I expect the original Americans to survive, but the question is how will they survive, as a shrinking minority as more and more of them migrate to mainstream society, continuing to live under the curse of reservation dependency on government and gambling money, however much of it is already at risk.

A journalist friend, after reading an early draft of this narrative, suggested that the punchline of my book presumably will offer a way out of the paradigm of victimhood and handouts. Sorry, friend. I don't have any bottom-line answer. The answer will have to come from the people themselves, just as all problems, big and small, are solved or not solved. And many Native Americans are dealing with the bigger issue, migrating from the reservation ghettos to the cities, achieving economic development where possible, addressing the alcohol scourge in some cases, adding attractions and accommodations at their casinos to go beyond gambling and make them destination places. But many tribes want to maintain their treaty right to dependence on government, some being too small or too remote to be viable on their own. And many seek to expand a dependence on gambling, often making direct payments to members from the profits, which do little to address long-range issues.

With all of that, will most of the original Americans succeed as self-sustaining members of the larger society, or will they continue to struggle

Afterword

along as its victims? I do not have the answer to that question, only hope for a positive answer.

Most "newcomers" to America do succeed in the larger society, as do many Native Americans. Most survive, but will they thrive as do so many immigrants? We'll see.

POSTSCRIPT

As I finish this narrative, I am struck by the endless efforts to "help the Indians," as well as efforts by tribes to get "help." First, the Federal Reserve Bank of Minneapolis announced it will start a national center to spur economic development on Indian reservations. Persistent poverty passed down through generations show the need for more research and energy toward community development, said the bank president. Two days later, a bipartisan delegation of three members of Congress showed up at the Leech Lake Indian Reservation in Minnesota to inspect the "shoddy learning environment" of its tribal high school. They promised to seek federal funding to improve that school and other poorly maintained Bureau of Indian Affairs schools, brought to light in a series of editorial articles by the Star Tribune of Minneapolis. Both relate to the dependency problem of Native Americans, defined as a curse in this book in the view of native leaders themselves. And it's a dependency, this author adds, still sought by some native tribes, such as the Pamunkeys of Virginia, who want federal recognition as a tribe—with a mere 200 members—to qualify for the benefits of that dependency. The tribe should qualify for approval, wrote the Washington Post, but that's not assured, partly because a casino operator fears competition for a planned gaming enterprise if the tribe establishes one of its own. And so it goes, on and on. Meantime, the age-old dispute of assimilation versus sovereignty underlies it all, as more and more natives move to the cities, many to live in poverty "ghettos," while a diminished number remains in reservation "ghettos," staunchly defending treaty rights to be sovereign nations.

ENDNOTES

Introduction

1. Interviews by the author with Seldon Kirk, Klamath Indian chairman, and with other members of the tribe, published in a series of articles in the Oregon Journal in Portland in August 1959, and cited throughout this book.
2. Yellow Horse Brave Heart, Maria, lead author of an essay on the historical trauma of native Americans, www.webpages.uidaho.edu.
3. Tribal mission, in Klamath tribes.org website.
4. From website www.indianaffairs.state.mn.us/tribes_shakopee.
5. Treuer, David, *Rez Life*, New York: Grove, 2012, p. 284.
6. "$1 million Each Year for All, Until Tribe's Luck Runs Out, *New York Times*, Aug. 9, 2012.

Chapter I. Independent

1. Peter Skene Ogden's Snake Country Journal 1826-27, Ex. No. 305, Oregon Historical Society Quarterly, Vol. II, 4910.
2. Annual Report of the Commissioner of Indian Affairs, transmitted to the 33rd U.S. Congress, 1854, from the National Archives.
3. Much of the description of the early life of the Klamaths is found in Anthropologist Theodore Stern's seminal book, *The Klamath Tribe, A People and Their Reservation*. Seattle: University of Washington Press, 1965.

4. Report of the Commissioner of Indian Affairs, 1864, from the National Archives.
5. Report of the Commissioner of Indian Affairs, 1863,. from the National Archives.
6. Landrum, Francis, *Guardhouse, Gallows and Graves.* Klamath Falls: Klamath County Museum, 1988, p. 9.
7. American-Indian Wars, from the internet site, http://www.history.com/topics/American-indian-wars"www.history.com/topics/American-indian-wars.
8. Report of the Commissioner of Indian Affairs, 1862, from the Natiional Archives.
9. Economic Self-Sufficiency Plan for the Klamath Tribes, prepared by the Klamath Tribes ESSP Committee, Chiloquin, 1992, p. 7.
10. Fixico, Donald L., *Termination and Relocation, Federal Indian Policy, 1945-1960.* Albuquerque: University of New Mexico Press, 1986, p. xi.
11. Report of the Commissioner of Indian Affairs, 1864, from the National Archives.
12. Stern, p. 36.
13. Commissioner of Indian Affairs, 1864.
14. Treaty between the United States of America and the Klamath and Modoc Tribes and the Yahooskin Band of Snake Indians, 1864, from Howe, Carrol, *Unconquered Uncontrolled, the Klamath Indian Reservation,* Bend: Maverick Publications Inc, 1992, p. 152.
15. Commissioners of Indian Affairs, 1863, 1864.
16. Ibid, 1864.
17. Stern, p. 27.
18. Ibid, p. 29.
19. Ibid, p. 33.
20. Ibid, p. 8.
21. Ibid, p. 39.
22. *The First Oregonians,* Corvallis: Oregon State University Press, 2007, p. 153.
23. "Modoc Indian Chief Signs His Mark Night Before Execution," Klamath Falls Herald and News, Oct. 21, 2011.

Endnotes

24. Interviews by this author with Lynn Schonchin on April 18, 2000, Nov. 1, 2011, and June 14, 2012.
25. Commissioner of Indian Affairs, 1962.
26. White, Richard, *The Roots of Dependency,* Lincoln: University of Nebraska Press, 1983, p. 59.
27. White, p. 120.
28. Commissioner of Indian Affairs, 1964.
29. Stern, p. 49.

Chapter II. Dependent

1. Howe, p. 154.
2. Ibid, p. 151-154.
3. Oregon Department of Fish and Wildlife et al, vs. Klamath Indian Tribe, U.S Court of Appeals, Ninth Circuit, 1985, p. 776.
4. *The First Oregonians,* p. 153.
5. Treuer, p. 38.
6. Declaration of Jeff Mitchell in lawsuit, The Klamath Tribes. vs. United States of America et al, U.S. District Court of Oregon, 1996.
7. United States of America vs. Adair et al, U. S. Court of Appeals, Ninth Circuit, 1983, p. 1409.
8. Declaration of Craig Bienz and other filings in the lawsuit, Klamath Tribes vs. United States of America et al, 1996.
9. United States vs. Adair, p. 1410.
10. Oregon Department of Fish and Wildlife, p. 777.
11. Stern, p. 58.
12. Ibid.
13. Ibid., p. 58.
14. Ibid., p. 41.
15. Ibid.

16. David Bunting and W.T. Trulove, *The Economic Impact of Federal Indian Policy: Incentives and Response of the Klamath Indians,* Eugene and Cheney: University of Oregon and Eastern Washington State College, Departments of Economics, 1971.

17. Ibid., p. 3.

18. Oregon Superintendent of Indian Affairs, 1863.

19. Ibid.

20. Stern, p. 44.

21. David Bunting and W.T. Trulove, *Some Experiences with Guaranteed Incomes and Lump Sum Payment4,* Eugene and Cheney: University of Oregon and Eastern Washington State College, Departments of Economics, 1970, p. 5.

22. Stern, p. 50.

23. Ibid, p. 49

24. From website, www.gbgm-umc.org/cooksonhillscenter/the-cherokee.htm.

25. Ibid., p. 97.

Chapter III. Independent?

1. Stanford Research Institute, *Preliminary Planning for Termination of Federal Control Over the Klamath Indian Tribe,* Palo Alto: April 1956.

2. Trulove and Bunting, *The Economic Impact of Federal Indian Policy,* p. 11.

3. Trulove, *The Economics of Paternalism* Cheney, Eastern Washington State College, Department of Economics, 1973, p. 7.

4. Dr. Calvin Hunt, *Klamath Tribes-a Sovereign Nation on the Dole,* from Herald and News, Klamath Falls, Oregon, Nov. 21, 2003, www.newswithviews.com/guest-opinion/guest13.

5. Truelove, Bunting, *Experiences…Economic Impact,* Ibid.

6. *Charles Trimble: Lessons from the Mashantucket Pequot Tribe,* anz.com/ www.indianz.com, and an email to the author, June 18, 2012.

7. *Gunman's tribe left with no answers,* Portland: The Oregonian, Oct. 29, 2014, p. a14, and various other sources through Google on the internet.

Endnotes

8. Rawls, James J., *Chief Red Fox is Dead*, New York: Harcourt Brace College Publishers, 1996, p. 59.

9. Native Nations Institute for Leadership, Management and Policy, University of Arizona, *Per Capita Distributions of American Indian Tribal Revenues*, University of Arizona, November 2007.

10. Tim Giago exchange of emails with author, June 5,6, 2012.

11. Indian Country Today Media Network.com, Aug. 28, 2013; The Republic azcentral.com, First Navaho casino in Arizona opens, May 24, 2013.

12. Native Nations Institute, Ibid; *Gambling has given Ho-Chunk New Hope*, Wisconsin Media Watch.org., March 2014.

13. Sioux City Journal.com, *Nebraska high court nixes gambling measure*, Sept. 5, 2014.

14. Gwynne, S.C., *Empire of the Summer Moon*, pps. 260-262.

15. Gerald Vizenor exchange of emails with author, May, June 2012.

16. Stern, Ibid., p. 190.

17. Klamath Tribes vs. United States of America, *Forest Management and Administration of Timber Sales at Klamath Indian Reservation*, Defendants Requested Findings of Fact, Volumn II, Indian Claims Commission, Feb. 2, 1977.

18. Klamath Tribes vs. United States of America, Indian Claims Commission, Feb. 25, 1974, p. 3118.

19. Trulove and Bunting, The Economic Impact, Ibid., p. 7.

20. Klamath Tribes vs. United States of America, *Forest Management…* Ibid. p. 13.

21. Trulove, email message to author, May 31, 2012.

22. Klamath Tribes vs. United States of America, Indian Claims Commission, No. 100, Amended Petition, Aug. 10, 1951, p. 6.

23. Klamath Tribes vs. United States of America, Filings with the Indian Claims Commission, Dec. 17, 1975, Oct. 14, 1977, and with the U.S. Claims Court, Dec. 20, 1982.

24. Seldon Kirk and Jesse Kirk, letter to the superintendent of the Klamath Reservation. Feb. 20, 1947.

25. Stern, p. 148.

26. Ibid., p. 153.

27. Ibid., p. 201, 240.

28. Barbara Alatorre interviews by the author, Sept. 30, Oct. 3, Oct. 6, 2011.

29. Phil Tupper interview by author Roberta Ulrich, Sept. 17, 18, 2002.

30. Klamath Tribes vs. United States of America, before Indian Claims Commission, Defendant Proposed Findings of Fact, Sept. 17, 1976, p. 22.

31. Richard Ferraro, Appeal Deciding Officer, Deputy Regional Forester, U.S. Forest Service, letter to Edmund Goodman, Native American Program, Oregon Legal Services, Portland, Oregon, and Patti Goldman, Earthjustice Legal Defense Fund, Seattle, Washington, Dec. 17, 1997.

32. Stern, Ibid., p. 262.

33. B. G. Courtright, Superintendent, U.S. Indian Agency, Klamath Agency, Oregon, Feb. 21, 1944, p. 17.

34. Klamath Reservation Planning Program, submitted to Congressional Subcommittee on Indian Affairs., March 25, 1944, p. 51.

35. Reservation planning, Klamath Reservation Program, Klamath Agency, Oregon, p.16.

36. Klamath Tribes vs. USA, Defendant Proposed Findings of Fact, Ibid., p. 22.

37. Courtright, Ibid.

38. Reservation Planning, Ibid. (The government and Klamath planning documents are both included in files listed in footnotes 32-34.)

39. Termination of Federal Supervision over the Klamath Indian Reservation, issued by the Oregon State Department of Education, Dec. 31, 1956, pps. 16-17.

Chapter IV. Terminated

1. Haynal, Patrick, *From termination through restoration and beyond: Modern Klamath cultural identity*, University of Oregon, 1994, p. 97.

2. Fixico, Donald, *Termination and Relocation: Federal Indian Policy, 1945-1960*, University of New Mexico Press, Albuquerque, 1986, p. 188.

Endnotes

3. Termination, An account of the termination of the Klamath Reservation from the Tribes' Point of View, Herald and News, Klamath Falls, Oregon, Oct. 13, 1999, p. 6.

4. Lynn Schonchin interviews, Ibid.

5. Interview with Jeff Mitchell by author Roberta Ulrich, Sept. 16, 2002.

6. Brown, Charles Crane, an examination of data generated since termination of the Klamath reservation, Ph.D. dissertation, University of Oregon, Eugene, 1973.

7. Report of Seattle Regional Office Federal Trade Commission, Consumer Problems of the Klamath Indians A Call for Action, October 1978, pps. 5, 8.

8. This section on Thomas Ball is based on interviews by authors Ulrich and Rigert dating from 2001 to 2012, email exchanges with Rigert in 2011, the Klamath News newsletter of the Klamath tribe in 1999 and Ball's doctoral dissertation of December 1998.

9. Klamath Tribes. vs. United States of America, before Indian Claims Commission, Defendant's Brief, Oct. 1, 1977.

10. Northwest Economic Associates, *Economic Studies in Support of Klamath Tribes' Self-Sufficiency and Impacts of Termination*, March 16, 1994, p. 25.

11. Frazier, Joseph, *Klamath Tribes reject land proposal*, The Oregonian, Oct. 15, 2003.

Chapter V. Casino Dependency

1. Bob Drury and Tom Clavin, *The Heart of Everything That Is, The Untold Story of Red Cloud, An American Legend,* Simon & Schuster, New York, 2013, p. 77.

2. Brown, Curt, *A Man Lost in History, the Darkest Chapter in Minnesota's Past, Through the Rise and Fall of One Dakota Leader,* Star Tribune, Minneapolis, series of six articles, Aug. 12-16, 2012.

3. *SMS Casino Millionaire Can't Afford to Pay his Victim's Family,* ://www.newsfornatives.com/"www.NewsForNatives.com; Frederick Melo, *Casino Millionaire Laughs Off Lawsuit,* Pioneer Press, St. Paul, Minnesota, March 8, 2010.

4. United States of America vs. Rueben Crowfeather, sentencing hearing before U.S. District Court Judge Michael Davis, Sept. 6, 2006.

5. In the Marriage of: Alan Welch, and Mary M. Welch, Memorandum Opinion and Order, before Judge Henry Buffalo, Court of Appeals of the Shakopee Mdewakanton Sioux (Dakota) Community.

6. *SMS Casino Millionaire,* Ibid., and In the Marriage of Alan Welch, Ibid.

7. Steve Date and Sharon Schmickle, series of five articles on Minnesota gaming, on www.Minnpost.com.

8. Sylvia Cohen vs. Little Six Inc., d/b/a Mystic Lake Casino, before Minnesota Court of Appeals, dissenting opinion by Judge James Randall, p. D10.

9. Brown, Curt, *Throngs Remember Stanley Crooks,* Star Tribune, Minneapolis, Minnesota.

10. Smith, Sue, supervisor, Little Six casino at Mystic Lake gambling enterprise, *Indian Gaming: Social Impacts of Little Six Casino on Shakopee Mdewakanton Sioux,* Wiki.umn.edu/pub/Amin3301.

11. *New York Times,* Ibid.

12. Indian Affairs Council, Ibid.; Molly Young, *A Tribal Force in Finance,* Star Tribune, Aug. 15, 2010.

13. Treuer, Ibid., p. 248.

14. National Gambling Impact Study Commission, Native American Gaming, www.govinfo.library.unt.edu/ngisc/research/nagaming.html.

15. Blount, Rachel, *A significant infusion of tribal funds has dramatically changed the racing landscape at Canterbury Downs,* Star Tribune, May 17, 2013.

16. *Tribe's giving falls off; rank stays high,* Star Tribune, Nov. 13, 2011.

17. The Klamath Tribes, Notes to the financial statements for the year ended Dec. 31, 2009.

18. Hallenbeck, Brian, *Nashantuckets end payments to tribal members,* The Day, March 2, 2012.

19. Donald Barlett and James Steele, *Special Report4 Indian Casinos,* Part 1, Time Magazine, December 2002.

20. Peterson, David, *Shakopee tribe offers a peek into its financial might,* Star Tribune, Jan. 11, 2012.

21. Onishi, Norimitsu, *Lucrative gambling pits tribe against tribe, The* New York Times, Aug. 8, 2012; Other information for this section comes from scattered news reports.

Endnotes

22. McGee, Leland, *Greed, Corruption and Indian Country's New Welfare State*, Indian Country Today, www.medianetwork.com, *June 27, 2013*.

23. Wilkins, David, *Two Possible Paths Forward for Native Disenrollees and the Federal Government?* Indian Country Today Media Network, June 4, 2013.

24. Cattelino, Jessica, *Fungibility: Florida Seminole Casino Dividends and the Fiscal Politics of Indigeneity,* American Anthropologist, Vol. III, Nov. 2, June 2009.

25. Native Nations Institute for Leadership, Management and Policy, The University of Arizona, *Per Capita Distributions of American Indian Tribal Revenues,* November 2007.

26. Star Tribune, *Tribal Leader: New gambling will harm Ojibwe, April 5, 2011;* Star Tribune, *Marge Anderson made history leading Ojibwe, July 1, 2013;* MinnPost website, Steve Date, *Flood of casino money brings challenges—and opportunities—for reservation schools,* Third of five articles starting Dec. 10, 2012.

27. Gonzales, Angela, "Gaming and displacement: winners and losers in American Indian casino development," 2003, published for UNESCO by Blackwell Publishing Ltd., Oxford, UK.

Chapter VI. Klamaths Today

1. Trulove, Bunting, Economic Impact, Ibid., p. 20.

2. "Regular" Tribal Council Meeting, March 9, 2011.

3. The Klamath Tribe, General Council Minutes, April 30, 1988.

4. Klamath Tribes vs. U.S. Forest Service, Declaration of Craig Bienz, April 4, 1996.

5. The Klamath Tribes, Tribal Council, Resolution #2013-33, Aug. 28, 2013.

6. Klamath General Council Minutes, April 30, 1988, Ibid.

7. Ibid.

8. Regular council meeting, March 9, 2011, Ibid.

9. Bettles, Lynn, *"Did you know April was National Alcohol Awareness Month—Honoring a Special Young Man,"* Klamath News, March/April 2011.

10. National Institute on Alcohol Abuse and Alcoholism, No. 18 PH 357, The Genetics of Alcoholism, July 1982.

11. White, Ibid. p. 211.
12. Status report: Chiloquin, Herald and News, Ibid., April 12, 2012.
13. Klamath Tribes Projects, Herald and News, Ibid, March 2, 2010, p. 5.
14. The Klamath Tribes, Economic Self-Sufficiency Plan, 1992.
15. Self-Sufficiency Plan, Ibid., Oct. 31, 2000.
16. "Sen. Ron Wyden says too costly for Congress," NW Public Radio at Washington State University, June 20, 2013, Nwpr.org/post/wyden.
17. Kelly, Bliss and Gosnell, *The political ecology of tribal land reacquisition*, Journal of Political Ecology 2113 Vol. 20.
18. Tims, Dana, The Oregonian, *Klamath Tribes seek 385 acres near Wilsonville, Sept. 11, 2009*, OregonLive.com.
19. Juillerat, Lee, *Gary Frost takes post as Klamath Tribes' chairman*, Herald and News, Ibid., Oct. 22, 2010.
20. Juillerat, Lee, Associated Press, *Modoc Nation moves forward in break with Klamath Tribes*, August 2010.

Chapter VII. Conclusion

1. Email from Thomas Ball, Ibid., March 30, 2012.
2. Rawls, Ibid., pps. 61, 110.
3. Wilkinson, Charles, *Blood Struggle The Rise of Modern Indian Nations*, W. W. Norton & Company, New York, 2005, p. 197.
4. Rawls, Ibid., pps. 58, 59.
5. The Associated Press, *Jewell makes emotional Pledge to Native Americans*, KTVN Channel 2, Reno, Nevada, June 27, 2013.
6. Lawrence, William, Speech at American Indian Law and Policy Symposium, University of Oklahoma, Norman, Oklahoma, March 21, 1998, from Native American Press/Ojibway News, Bemidji, Minnesota.
7. Doyle, Pat, *Chip Wadena, longtime head of White Earth band, dies at 75*, Star Tribune, Minneapolis, Minnesota, June 24, 2014.
8. Pritchard, Justin, The Associated Press, *Tribes mishandle funds with few consequences*, from The Oregonian, Portland, Oregon, Oct. 8, 2013.

Endnotes

9. Stephen Cornell and Joseph Kalt, *Sovereignty and Nation-Building*, The Harvard Project on American Indian Economic Development, 2003.

10. Fixico, Ibid., p. 203.

11. Morrison, Scott Kayla, Attorney at Law, *The Big Lie, the Reality*, from Native American Press, March 1, 1996.

12. Castle, Steven, *Caribbean Nations Seek Slavery Reparations, Citing Lasting Harm*, The New York Times, Oct. 21, 2013.

13. White, Ibid. p. 204.

14. Randall, Judge James, *Camp Justice v. White Clay*, Undated.

15. Row, Jess, *Without Reservation*, The New York Times, Nov. 25, 2012.

16. Cornell, Ibid.

17. Treuer, Ibid. p. 248.

18. Bilefsky, Dan, *Are the Roma primitive or Just Poor?*, The New York Times, Oct. 20, 2013.

19. Rincon Lopez, Debra, posting on Maqlaqs Hemcunga (people talking).Com/apps/profile/47019871/

20. From https://en.wikipedia.org/wiki/Pine_Ridge_Indian_Reservation

21. Drury and Clavin, Ibid. p. 11.

22. Obituary, Edison P. Chiloquin, Herald & News, Klamath Falls, Oregon, May 25, 2003.

23. Klamath Tribes, "Special" General Council Meeting minutes, Sept. 28, 2013.

CPSIA information can be obtained
at www.ICGtesting.com
Printed in the USA
FSHW010738140221
78618FS